Messages from Shiva vol. 2

Channeled by River Lightbearer

In collaboration with Shiva, a being of light

Cover by Kim Ramsey-Winkler

Published by:

Vegan Wolf Productions
veganwolfproductions@gmail.com

CONTENTS

RIVER'S INTRODUCTION

In 2006, I learned how to channel my guide, a being of light called Shiva. For a few years after that, I offered channeling sessions in a metaphysical store as well as doing both paid and free channeling on online forums and by email.

In 2009, a client booked a session with me at the store. He had seen that I channeled a being called Shiva and, logically, believed I channeled *the* Shiva. As in the Hindu deity. The client appeared to be a Caucasian American man but was also a Shaivite Hindu, and he wanted to talk to the deity he worshipped.

At the time, my Shiva was still refusing to tell me whether or not he was the deity, though he had explained a few times that many deities in polytheistic religions and spiritual paths are actually beings of light or other beings of high energetic vibration. He did this partly to try to help break my tendency to believe I needed to know everything and partly because he wanted me to believe and accept that I was "worthy" of channeling him.

When I arrived at the store and the owner introduced me to the client, I clarified for him that I channeled a being of light, not necessarily the deity he wanted to speak with. He seemed to accept that, so we went into the reading room. I entered trance and Shiva greeted the client…and things went sideways.

The client spoke Hindi. A language with which I have no familiarity. And although Shiva is capable of understanding languages other than the ones I speak, trying to force that understanding and the ability to speak another language through my energy system could have harmed me. This is the case with any knowledge; although the beings who work with humans have access to a very broad range of knowledge, when we channel, the beings are constrained to some extent by our limitations. They could force information, but that would have a detrimental impact on our energy systems, so they generally won't do so.

When my client started speaking Hindi, I started to panic. This wasn't visible to him, of course; I was in trance and he was interacting directly with Shiva. But Shiva was aware. He tried to calm me down while also speaking to the client to explain the issue and request that the client confine himself to speaking English for the duration of the session.

The client again seemed to accept this. He switched to English and asked his question again. But the damage was done. I was terrified that he would think I was a fraud because of the language thing. I, obviously, didn't know the answer to his question, and that freaked me out also even though I wasn't the one responding and therefore didn't need to know. I broke trance, apologized to the client, and took him to the checkout counter to get a refund.

That was the last time I tried channeling for over a decade. I was so convinced the client believed me to be a fraud and would tell others I was faking it that I stopped even admitting I channeled. I didn't stop speaking to Shiva and my other guides, but I stopped speaking *about* them.

In 2016, when I was given the charge to start my business RiverEvolutions (at the time called River Flow Healing), I chose to only offer energy healing. That was a skill I also hadn't practiced in several years, so I needed to restore my knowledge of it, but I was more comfortable with it. There were set techniques, I had the manual to study so I could refresh my memory, and I didn't have any mental or emotional baggage around it because I hadn't had any negative experiences with clients in the past. I wasn't completely confident in my skills, but I was far more confident and less afraid of being called a fraud than when it came to channeling.

Later that year, I attempted something I called "guided readings" (a/k/a relayed channeling) at a nearby metaphysical store. Instead of entering trance to provide channeling for clients, I remained conscious and simply told the clients what Shiva was saying. That didn't work as well as I would have liked.

Sometimes I had difficulty hearing Shiva, and sometimes I was hesitant to pass along his exact words out of concern that the client might be upset or angry about what Shiva was saying, but for the most part the sessions went smoothly. I had one client who vehemently denied everything Shiva and I said, but that didn't faze me as much as it would have in the past. I simply ended the session and asked the cashier to give her a refund. He and I processed together after she left, and he confirmed that I was not a fraud and said he believed the client had reacted the way she had because I'd struck a nerve, not because Shiva or I was wrong.

After a few months, though, for various reasons including travel distance, I chose to stop working with that store. I still wasn't offering channeling of any type to individual clients through my business. I still was too afraid to do so. Until 2019, I continued officially only offering energy healing sessions, though at times I did informally channel for people who had questions or as part of a healing session.

In 2019, after discussions with Shiva and my other guides and with my partner, I decided to take the leap into offering channeling again. I did a few "beta test" sessions with people I trusted, and those went well, though some of those clients opted not to give me the feedback they'd promised, and none decided to have additional sessions with me. I also had someone approach me to do a paid email channeling for them, and although I felt it went well and that I'd given them the information they wanted and needed, they declined to give me any feedback or even their thoughts on what I'd told them. Without having any indication from people I'd worked with as to whether I was channeling accurately and effectively, I held back from wholeheartedly offering it or even admitting I did it.

I plodded on through the rest of 2019 offering energy healing sessions and instruction and hoping that eventually I would feel comfortable channeling. Shiva didn't pressure me in the slightest; although he expressed that he looked forward to working with me in that way again, he wanted me to make the decision based on what I wanted and needed, not on his wishes. As someone who had become all too accustomed to being forced to make choices on the basis of other people's wants rather than my own needs, I appreciated that Shiva was willing to give me time and space to determine for myself whether channeling was something I really wanted to do.

Toward the end of 2019, I bought a car that actually ran without needing vast amounts of repairs. In order to finance it, I chose to start driving for Lyft. This was much more lucrative than RiverEvolutions, and although I continued working with my existing students, I stopped putting much energy into the business. I still wanted to earn a living from energy healing and channeling, but the reality at that point was that I wasn't bringing in much if any income from those things, while I was bringing in enough from Lyft to start paying down and even paying off credit cards and other debt. Again, I kept up with studies and personal practices that facilitated my abilities as an energy healing practitioner, and I continued speaking with my guides, but my energy and focus were diverted.

And then 2020 happened.

I'm sure I don't need to explain the previous sentence. For me, global events meant driving Lyft came to an end, because I was not comfortable having strangers getting in and out of my car when there was no way to tell whether they were sick—or whether I was. It meant I turned my focus back to RiverEvolutions, but not with the right mindset; my thinking was that with everything going on in the world, of course people would benefit from energy healing services, but part of my mind was also stuck on the idea that without income from Lyft, I had to make money somehow, and the only other thing I could do was energy healing.

Obviously this is not the most beneficial energy to bring to any sort of business, especially one that involves serving others. I didn't gain any clients. In fact, even reactions and responses I'd been getting on social media dried up. Instead of attracting aligned people to work with me, I was repelling pretty much everyone. In 2020, for the first time since 2015, I had no income at all from my business.

What I did gain that year was a deeper connection with myself and the time to address issues and unhealed aspects I'd been ignoring in favor of trying to do things for other people.

There were no other people for me to do things for. I kept in touch with my kids, but one of them lived with their fiancé and friends of the family, so had plenty of support, and the other moved to another country for graduate school halfway through the year. My husband withdrew even more than usual and primarily wanted to be left alone, and while I was able to keep in touch with my partner by phone and occasionally video call, we only saw each other sporadically out of concerns about the health of other people in our households. For the first time in my life, I was able to devote the majority of my time, energy, and focus to taking care of myself and actually figuring out who I was and who I wanted to be.

As I put more energy and focus into my own healing and spiritual growth, I began to feel more and more as if I wanted—and needed—to offer channeling as well as energy healing. Maybe even instead of energy healing, since I had started feeling as if I wasn't effectively serving people through that practice. Shiva and I discussed this over time, and during that summer, we decided I would start sharing a daily channeled message on Facebook, both for practice in channeling and to indicate to others that it was something I did. I posted the first message on August 3, 2020.

However, I didn't share these messages with the intention or energy of attracting clients. That was something I hoped for, but my focus was on simply channeling the messages and having the confidence to post them without fear of what other people might think. If the messages didn't resonate for some people, they could ignore them; if people thought I was "crazy" or had other negative opinions, I could ignore those. In addition to the messages, I started talking and posting more about channeling and how working with my guides had helped me through some of the most difficult times in my life.

My guides continued supporting me as I underwent surgery that led to a cancer diagnosis, which strengthened my resolve to actually and honestly progress in my healing journey and create a life for myself that felt fulfilling and beneficial. (The cancer was entirely removed in the surgery, and I required no further treatment.) They supported me as I continued examining the aspects of myself and beliefs and assumptions that were holding me back, and as I chose to take the leap into actually working on those things instead of trying to pretend they weren't problems.

I was still reluctant to offer channeling, but eventually I could no longer ignore the strong call I felt to make that service available. I started doing live and recorded videos in which I channeled, and I shared these on Facebook and YouTube. I started talking to people about channeling and my guides. Through the work 2020 allowed me to do on myself and my own healing, I developed the confidence and determination to stop hiding and be who I actually was, doing what I actually did.

In early 2021, I was feeling constrained and desperate for a change of scenery, especially since my husband had taken a temporary layoff from work and so he and I were home together all day every day. I love my husband, but neither of us is particularly good at or comfortable with constant interaction with other humans, even each other. During the first month of the year, we battled Covid, with his symptoms becoming bad enough that he almost needed hospitalization, while I remained asymptomatic. This increased the friction between us, since for two solid weeks neither of us could set foot outside our apartment since there was no way to exit without being in common areas of our building.

Once we were both recovered, I decided to leave for a few weeks. I needed space and so did my husband, and fortunately for me, my committed partner owns a house in Florida, a place he'd taken me to a couple of times and where I felt at home and comfortable. My partner gave me the go-ahead, and I took off to Florida.

That was where my journey took its next steps. By "accident" while visiting Cocoa Village, I found a metaphysical store and started talking to one of the owners about the channeling I do and who my guide is. She paused for a moment, chuckled a bit, and asked if she could tell me what her guides were saying. When I consented, she told me that Shiva wasn't the guide I would continue to channel; I would be channeling a guide of higher vibration and would be working closely with him going forward.

I was a little uncertain, partly because some of her phrasing sounded a bit ego-stroking to me, so I thanked her and, on the way back to the house, asked Shiva for confirmation. He said that yes, the woman and her guides were telling the truth, and that I had already been speaking with the being they referred to. He said he would continue to work with me, but I would transition to channeling the other being.

That being, Pietkela, first evidenced himself to me toward the end of my marriage to my children's father, not long after I initially learned to channel. For fifteen years, I had greeted him every morning when I greeted the beings I recognized as my guides, and we had occasionally had other conversations as well. But I did not know, until this day in March 2021, that Pietkela was not only one of my guides but was the being I would transition to channeling.

As of this writing, I channel both Shiva and Pietkela, though not simultaneously. Each of them has their areas of expertise, understanding, and interest, so there are times when Shiva is more beneficial for a client than Pietkela would be or vice versa. Pietkela also has not worked as extensively with humans in general or with me specifically as Shiva has, and his bluntness and obvious lack of humanness are difficult for some people to deal with. This means Shiva, with his warmth and ability to at least present in a more human way, is a better option.

As part of the transition, we decided that the daily channeled messages would come from Pietkela rather than Shiva. The last month of Shiva's messages was May, 2021. Since I had already compiled many of his messages into a book and was planning a follow-up, I chose to move forward with the compilation, the book you are now reading. This book includes only messages from Shiva, channeled from February 1 to May 29, 2021. (His messages from May 30 and 31 were explanations of the transition from him to Pietkela and a farewell to the people who had been reading the messages.) As with the first compilation, I have organized the messages by topic rather than presenting them in chronological order.

In the future, I will release compilations of Pietkela's messages. In the meantime, I hope Shiva's messages in this volume and the previous one will give you guidance and peace.

SHIVA'S INTRODUCTION

Greetings. I am called Shiva, though that is only one name by which humans have known me over the course of my work in your world.

For many of your centuries, that work has involved the Core Self of the human you may know as River Lightbearer, whom I know as Ganatram, a name I gave to them several of their lifetimes ago. They and I have worked in conjunction for their own healing and growth as well as to support other humans and to provide an outlet for myself and beings with whom I collaborate to share our knowledge and information with your world.

Over the time during which Ganatram and I have worked together in their current lifetime, we have found several ways in which they have shared my words. At times, they have resisted sharing at all, and this is something I have accepted, for I have no desire to force any human to do anything they do not wish to do. My primary focus in my work with Ganatram is to facilitate their own growth and healing, in whatever nonharmful means this may be done. Providing messages of support and healing to other humans is simply, as you might say, a bonus.

Most recently, I offered to Ganatram the possibility of sharing messages from me to a wider audience through online means. This appealed to them as they were struggling with the idea of working individually with other humans and were having difficulty in informing others of the services offered. Being able to simply type my words and post them online was, for them, an easier and more effective method.

We began this aspect of our work during the health crisis your world experienced at the turn of the decade. Channeling my messages offered Ganatram an outlet for creativity as well as an opportunity to practice and restore their skills in working with me. For my part, I was appreciative of the opportunity to share my words and to work more directly with Ganatram as they rebuilt the channeling skills they had let slide over several years. This is not a judgment of them, for it was necessary for them to set aside these skills for a time in order to attend to their own healing and growth, but the time during which they did not channel resulted in a loss of some level of skill which they wished to restore.

We found this work together both easy and difficult. Ganatram's fluidity in receiving and accurately conveying my messages grew beyond their previous skill level. It became easier for them to hear my words even when not in full trance, and easier for us to work in collaboration to present the messages in written form. At the same time, although Ganatram expressed excitement at the idea of sharing our messages to a wider audience, they feared the reactions of some of those who would see those messages.

Fear is often an obstacle for humans in their endeavors, and at times they are unaware of how blocked they have become. Ganatram was cognizant of the fact that they feared what others might say if they presented channeled messages, but it took time for them to overcome their resistance and accept that some people simply would not respond positively, and that this was not a statement about Ganatram or their validity, but rather about prejudices and preconceptions humans carry.

They began sharing these messages, and after several months concluded that to be of further service, they wished to compile the messages into book form. We worked together on this project as well, and the first such book was presented to the world in the spring of 2021. The book you are currently reading is the second compilation, for we continued working together to provide daily messages for some time longer.

I knew, as Ganatram and I began this aspect of our work, that it would be temporary. Although Ganatram was unaware that the being they know as Pietkela would become their primary guide and the one they would channel most often, this was knowledge I possessed. I could not share this information with Ganatram until such a time as they were ready to accept the change along with their own abilities and what humans might call "worth" to work with Pietkela and, through him, the collective of beings of which he is part.

When Ganatram was told of the impending change by the woman they encountered in Florida, it was because the time had come for us to make this transition. I assured Ganatram I would not be leaving them, for once a being is connected with and acts as guide to a human, the connection endures as long as the human wishes it to, though the being may remain in the background rather than working daily and overtly with the human.

While Ganatram was resistant to the idea of working with a being of higher energetic vibration than myself, since they had initially struggled even to believe they had a high enough vibration to work with me, they were more resistant to the possibility that I would desert them as many humans have done over the years. Once they were reassured that I would remain with them and would simply be working with them in a different capacity than previously, the transition became easier and they were more willing to work more closely with Pietkela.

Part of Pietkela's purpose in working with Ganatram is to offer messages to your world that will enable the next phase of your existence to begin and develop. These messages include talk of healing and balance, and of acceptance and the understanding that each person's journey is valid even if it is not the same as the journeys of others.

Because Pietkela's purpose is slightly different from mine and his messages were becoming more needed and relevant given what was occurring in your world, and because he was becoming

Ganatram's primary guide while I was moving to a different place in their life, the determination was made that the daily messages upon which Ganatram and I had worked would instead become a collaboration between them and Pietkela.

I have been pleased and honored to communicate with you through these messages and other means, and I continue to enjoy working with Ganatram to offer channeling to certain humans for whom I am better suited than Pietkela might be. Although I am no longer the author of the daily messages, I offer my previous messages to you through this book in the hope that they will bring you greater understanding of yourself and the issues currently facing your world, as well as the contributions you may, if you so choose, make to healing within your world and within yourself.

I am still present and still at times speak with humans, as well as speaking consistently with Ganatram, who has become my friend as well as the human I guide. Should you have questions raised by the words you read in these pages, you may choose to contact us to ask those questions or receive clarification of what I have stated. Additionally, the messages in this book contain my energy, and it is my hope that this will bring you peace.

Be well and be loved.

LOOKING WITHIN

For some of you, life has been a constant lesson in hiding and pretending. In obscuring who you are, not only from others but at times from yourself as well.

This is not a judgment, for you made those choices and learned that lesson to protect yourself against harm others may have inflicted upon you. This was not a conscious decision, but a protective mechanism created by your mind to keep you safe at times when safety did not exist.

If you are no longer in those times, those mechanisms no longer are required. Yet releasing them is not as simple as choosing. Just as you did not consciously create this protection, so it is difficult to consciously let it go. However, know that if you are in safety now, even if you do not fully perceive it, the time has come to release your mask. To cease pretending and begin the work of becoming your true self.

This work is not easy, yet it is abundantly rewarding, for each of you deserves to be who you truly are. This work may necessitate aid from others, and if you choose to begin the work and to request the aid, it shall be there for you.

You are wonderful. Do you not have a right to become the wonderful person you have always been?

How have you rejected the Self within you?

When one experiences harmful or painful incidents, at times the very aspect of the self that had this experience is buried and rejected. This is a mechanism for protection, but it causes further harm. If you reject part of yourself, how can others accept you fully?

This is not something you do intentionally, but it causes no less harm for its unintentional nature.

Learn to embrace yourself. The parts of you that have experienced harm and pain are there, waiting to be loved and embraced. This is not easy work, but for true healing to occur, it is necessary.

Know that you need not take on this work alone. Supports exist for you. Seek them, and accept aid when offered.

You are worthy of love. Will you give this gift to yourself?

In the dark time of the year, in the days when you must remain in your home due to cold and treacherous conditions, I invite you to explore yourself.

In the bustle of your daily life, you often neglect what lies within you. You obscure your inner self with activities and accomplishments. You erect a facade for the rest of the world to see, and it becomes so entrenched that you yourself believe the facade to be who you truly are.

Now is a time for reflection and deeper understanding of who you are. Now is a time to examine who you wish to become.

If you choose to take up this task, it may be difficult, for looking within may bring to light facets of yourself that you wish were not there or that are painful to face. Seek support when this occurs, for you do not undertake this alone. Those who love you are here for you.

Now is a time to know who you are. Will you choose this task?

Take time to be alone.

Often, humans fill their lives with activities and with other people. Being alone has become a lost art form as people have sought to fill time and avoid connection with the most important being in each life: the Self.

Spending time in solitude can be frightening at first, for it is a habit you have lost. Yet it can be incredibly beneficial as you seek to heal from your past and create a more positive life for yourselves, for how can you create your best self if you are unaware of who you are and who you wish to be?

It may be uncomfortable for you to spend time alone, but you are encouraged to accept that discomfort and seek the connection with yourself and the benefit it will provide.

Heed what your bodies tell you. Some of you have become disconnected from your physical forms, whether through trauma or simply unawareness. Some of you are connected, but ignore the sensations and messages your body sends.

When you are not caring for your physical form, you are not caring for yourself. Although this form is transient in the grand scheme of things, still it is the form in which you will pass this lifetime, and it benefits you to tend to what it tells you.

Refrain from ignoring pain or illness. Although for some, obtaining medical care is difficult or nearly impossible, if you are able to seek it do so when needed. At the least, allow yourself to rest and recover when injury or illness strikes.

You live within this form, and you know, although may not be fully conscious of it, when something is not right. Heed this, and care for yourself as you are able, for you deserve to be cared for and well.

For some of you, the concept of "being in your body" is terrifying. Your body has experienced harm. It has experienced pain. You have no wish to be in it.

For others, your body is not the correct one in which to dwell. It is not matched with who you truly are.

Your body is the container in which your soul has chosen to pass this lifetime. It can be altered, but still it is yours.

Your feelings about your body are also yours, and are valid. Yet I encourage you, as you are able, to befriend this physical form in which you live. Connect at least with the parts of it that do not cause you pain or fear. Connect with the sensations it experiences. Connect with it as an aspect of your core Self, for in some ways it is the physical manifestation of that Self, even if some pieces of it have manifested incorrectly.

I will not tell you to "love your body"; for some of you, this is not yet possible, and I will not tell you to do something which will cause you additional stress. I merely invite you to befriend at least the parts of your body which do not bring you pain, and to remember that while your body is a manifestation of you, you are not defined by it. At your core, you are your Self, wonderfully created.

Meeting your own needs does not detract from others. Tending to your health and well-being does not take away from anyone. But refusing your needs and ignoring your health will detract, for you are unable to fully care for others when you are not caring for yourself.

I do not speak of emotional caring, but of literal. If you are physically and mentally depleted owing to ignoring and denying your needs, how can you provide for another? If you constantly say yes to their requests and demands while saying no to your own, how can you effectively meet their requests?

In your life, you have chosen to prioritize certain people. These may be family members such as children or a spouse, or perhaps friends or colleagues. While in some cases, such as parenting, it is necessary to prioritize another, doing so at the cost of your own needs and health is not beneficial to them or to you.

While you do bear responsibility to some others, your first responsibility is to yourself. You need not ignore or negate their needs to meet your own, but if you ignore and negate your own, you cannot effectively meet theirs and may develop resentment toward them.

Tend to your needs so that you may aid others as you wish to do.

Why do you believe you were placed in this world? What do you believe to be your purpose?

I encourage you to examine this question within yourself, for some of you will initially give the answer that has been taught to you. The answer you have been conditioned to believe.

What others have placed upon you is not your purpose. Tending to others at the cost of caring for yourself is not your purpose. Ignoring your needs in favor of others' demands is not your purpose.

When you were born into your current form, your soul arrived with a chosen purpose. This is not something you are "assigned" or that is placed on you by any person or being; it is something you yourself chose at a soul level. This also does not mean you chose "lessons" or harm to learn and grow, for the actions of others are not something you choose. Rather, the purpose your soul chose is the work you wish to accomplish in this lifetime.

No matter what you have experienced in your life, your core Self still knows this purpose. Your knowledge has become obscured by what others have taught or done to you, but it is still there.

I encourage you to make contact with this knowledge. With your core Self. This may be done through meditation for those for whom meditation is possible, but that is not the only method. You may ask your guides for aid. You may work with a healer or other practitioner, or with a traditional professional. Or you may simply sit with yourself and see what comes to your mind.

Connecting with your soul and your purpose will help you progress, for it will show you what to bring into your life to facilitate that purpose, and these are the things that will bring you joy and fulfillment.

I encourage you today to find one small thing to do purely for your own benefit. One thing that will meet a need, or, better, a desire you have been neglecting.

Those who depend upon you or have come to expect you to be available for their every need and whim may protest against your choice to place yourself first today, but this is not your responsibility. They will not fall apart if you choose to spend a small amount of time tending to yourself and not to them, though they may attempt to convince you otherwise or your fears and ego may try to persuade you otherwise.

Others may be priorities in your life, but it will benefit you and them should you choose to place yourself first in your list of priorities, at least from time to time. Today is a time to make this choice.

You are important.

You are valued.

Without you, the Universe would not be as incredible as it is, for each individual life, each atom of existence, creates the glorious picture of the Whole. Were you not part of that picture, it would not be as it is.

Yet you doubt your importance. You devalue yourself. You believe others would be better off without you.

This is not to fault you. For some of you, this is not a chosen way of thinking, but a combination of what you have been conditioned to believe and disruptions in the workings of your mind that are beyond your control. I am not here to state that you must "think positively" or any of the other platitudes you may have heard, for we, the beings who work with you, recognize that you are not choosing this.

I am, rather, here to refute those beliefs you hold within.

You are important, even if you believe otherwise. You are valued, even if some in your life have devalued you. And you are needed in this world and this Universe.

It is my hope you will read these words and perhaps experience at least a glimmer of belief, for they are true.

Many of you fear change because what awaits on the other side is unknown to you. When you do not know for certain what will occur, your mind says, it may be negative. It may be harmful. You may become someone different, and you cannot conceptualize who that may be.

The unknown can be frightening, for it is unseen to most of you. Even those who purport to see the future see only potentials; the absolute future cannot be seen until it becomes the present, for the future is always alterable until it actually comes to be.

However, through your fear, know that you deserve abundance, and that the changes you undergo will ultimately lead you to this benefit. For some, the path will be winding and crooked and will at times turn back upon itself; for others, the path will be more straightforward. All, though, shall reach what awaits them, and for most, this shall be of great benefit.

Fearing the unknown is human nature, and I do not state that you must release this fear. Rather, I encourage you to acknowledge it and love the parts of yourself from which the fear is generated, for your love for yourself will help counter the fear and allow the changes to flow more easily.

Within you, you carry wonders. You hold skills and knowledge that are unique to you. Even if others have similar skills and knowledge, they cannot have exactly what you possess, for they are not you.

This unique perception and understanding you have of the world is desperately needed, for each individual contributes to the growth and progress of the Whole. You hide away out of fear of what other humans may say or do if you evidence yourself fully, yet the more you hide, the less those humans will learn of tolerance and beauty.

This is not to say that you are here to teach people tolerance. That phrasing is often used to minimize those who experience prejudice and harm, and we, the beings who work with and observe you, will never state that anyone must experience harm in order to learn or teach lessons. That is not how the Universe works.

Rather, when you exhibit tolerance for others who have not harmed you, and when you demonstrate a different way to see the world, some will learn from it, and this will bring improvement in the world. This may not be intentional work on your part, but simply you being yourself, as you may say.

Be yourself. Come out of hiding and show what you know. Share your gifts and skills. Share your perceptions of the world around you. From these, others will learn and grow simply by being exposed to what you offer.

You are not required to contort yourself to meet the needs of others. Some of you have structured your lives around providing what others need or wish from you, but this is not in service to them. They are not learning to provide for themselves, but rather expect you to do all for them while they do nothing.

More, providing for their needs in this manner is not in service to you. You are denying your own needs in favor of theirs. You are placing their desires over your health and well-being.

No matter what your role may be in the life of another, you are not solely responsible for meeting their needs or fulfilling their wishes. Placing yourself and your needs ahead of others at times is not selfishness, but self-care. You cannot effectively meet others' needs if you ignore your own.

Some of you have been taught that your only purpose for existing is to meet others' needs. This is untrue. Your purpose for existing is to learn and grow. To progress. To care for yourself. At times, providing for others is part of this path. But at other times, it is necessary to set a boundary against this pattern so that you may truly take care of your own needs and live a life which brings you healing and joy.

Selfishness is not desirable, but neither is pure selflessness. There is a middle ground, so to speak, and it is here that you and those you love will find the most benefit.

In your life, you have experienced the negation of your needs and of yourself as a person. Those who were meant to care for you have instead denied you the care you required. Those in whom you have come in contact have derided you and caused you to believe you are not worthy of care.

For some of you, the people who treated you in this manner are no longer present in your life. Yet you continue the treatment they inflicted. They are no longer present, but their voices and the effects of their behavior linger. You are now the one denying your needs and your worth.

I encourage you to examine the areas in which you are negating yourself. The needs you deny or refuse to meet. Examine what brings you joy, or what has the potential to bring joy should you choose to allow yourself to engage in it. Examine what you need in order to heal from your past and live a life of fulfillment rather than merely existing.

This is not easy work, for you have spent many years in negation and denial of your needs and of your worth. Yet to heal, you must acknowledge what is needed for healing to occur. You must recognize that you are worthy of healing and are abundantly deserving of having your needs met.

You are not alone in this work, but those who are with you to aid you cannot help until you are willing to do the work. I encourage you to begin.

You know yourself, and yet you doubt this knowledge. When another tells you who you are, tells you their perception of you, at times you internalize what they say.

This is unnecessary and is harmful to your sense of self. No one can tell you who you are. No one knows you better than you know yourself. Although you may have lost touch with this inner knowing, it still is there. You still know who you are.

Spend time engaging in self-study. As a child, you knew your true self, yet as you grew, others convinced you that you were wrong. Spend time now relearning what you knew as a child.

Nothing that has occurred in your life has taken away your ability to know your true self. Nothing has erased that self from existence. Experiences and the words of others may have obscured your true self, but they have not erased it.

Take this time. Reconnect with your core. Find the love within you once again.

EMBRACE YOUR INNER POWER

Your innate power is not something which you must be granted or allowed by another. It exists within you and always has. Yet many of you have lost touch with this. Many of you have lost touch with yourselves.

In your life journey, particularly when that journey involves healing from past experiences, being able to recognize and embrace your innate power is essential--and difficult. You may deny that the power exists or even fear its existence, and yet deep within, you know that it is there.

Open yourself to the power you have to create a life in which joy and abundance are present. Know that you have this power and you are deserving of these things in your life.

Some of you have experienced the removal of your power, either by force or because you saw no other option.

It is time now to realize that this power was never truly removed from you. It has merely been hidden, obscured by those events and by those people who brought you harm.

They have not taken away who you are at your core. That core Self is something which no one can take from you, and it is in this core that your true power dwells.

Begin now to connect with that Self. You may believe you have already done so, but if you continue to reject or deny your inner power, that connection is not strong and needs strengthening.

Begin now to strengthen this connection, even if you fear becoming who you truly wish to be.

When one has experienced the abuse of power by others, having power feels overwhelming and terrifying. You have seen power abused, and so cannot conceive of power being beneficial.

Know that those who have abused their power, who have claimed power over you, were in the wrong. True power does not come from the subjugation of others, but from the owning and accepting of responsibility and abilities within oneself.

You fear accepting your inner power because you fear abusing it, but this is unlikely to occur. You know how it feels to have another abuse power over you. You are able to make a different choice with your own power.

Power comes from within and is dependent upon what lies within. Within you lies a Self which wishes no harm to others, nor to you. It is from this Self that your power will arise when you are willing to accept it.

Within you is an immense well of power. How you use this power is up to you. Know that this power is not something to fear, or something about which to distrust yourself. It is the power to become. To grow. To heal.

As you progress in your life and in your healing journeys, for each of you is on such a journey though perhaps for different reasons, you may draw upon this power to choose your steps. To learn to trust and embrace yourself. To find others to support you as you also may support them.

Release your fears of this power, for it is not something which works against you, but something you may use in your work for yourself. It is part of your Self, and it is there to aid you.

Some of you turn to others to "learn" how to wield your creative power. You turn to those who name themselves spiritual leaders to learn what you "should" create.

It is not inherently unwise to seek guidance from other sources, but at times, you accept their guidance even when your inner guidance, the knowledge of your Core Self, contradicts it.

You, at your core, know more than you realize. You know who you truly are, even if you have not yet attained conscious awareness of this knowledge. You know what will most benefit you and lead you to a life in which you achieve your highest ideal.

When your inner voice speaks to you, whether this "speaking" is literal or takes another form such as a "sinking feeling" or other indication that something is not right, heeding it will lead you further into your most beneficial life. Ignoring it will lead only to continued struggle as you attempt to force yourself into the restrictions created by those you try to follow.

Even genuinely benevolent leaders and practitioners cannot speak to what is best for all. They speak only from their own experiences and what has worked for them. If your inner knowledge tells you that it will not work for you, heed this, and know that it is not a flaw within you that prevents others' methods from working for you. It is simply that you are not them, and what works for them does not work for you. It is difference, not fault or flaw.

Heed your inner guidance even over the words of this message, for your core Self knows what is true for you.

Other people's beliefs do not define you.

Other people's behavior toward you, their words, their insults, do not define you.

Yet these things can bring harm. In your world, some are fond of reciting a rhyme about “sticks and stones.” According to the words of this rhyme, words do not hurt.

This is false. Indeed, words may bring more and longer-lasting pain and harm than physical attacks.

Others’ words do not define you. What they believe about you does not create who you are. Yet you feel pain about their words and beliefs, and this is valid. All emotions which you feel in response to others’ hatred are valid.

Even words spoken to you as a child by other children can have vast, long-ranging effects depending upon the context in which and the frequency with which they were spoken. And this, too, is valid, for receiving hatred and painful words as a child from other children on a regular basis can be as traumatic as abuse or assault.

You need not allow others to tell you to “let go” of these words. You need not accept contempt or negative comments from others who believe you are “wallowing” or “whining” when you speak of the effects people’s beliefs and words have had upon you.

Yet you also need not allow the others who have spoken harm to you to define you. Pain can leave scars, but those scars do not create your Core Self. They are part of you, but they are not you.

You are the sole possessor of the right and power to define who you are. I encourage you to remember and claim this power.

For some of you, trusting yourselves and your inner guidance and power is among the most difficult tasks you face. You have learned over time and through detrimental experiences that you are not to be trusted, for you believe that you have caused the harm which has been inflicted upon you.

For some of you, the belief that you caused and controlled this harm is empowering and has led you to positive creations. I do not wish to negate this, for it is a truth and a source of beneficial power for you.

However, for others, this belief holds you back. You fear making any move to improve your life out of the mistaken belief that you might cause further harm to yourself or to others. Your belief that you created harm leads you to believe that harm is all you are capable of creating.

Nothing could be further from the truth. You did not create this harm, for you did not create the impulse within others to cause harm. You are not to blame for the actions of those who make these choices.

Your inner power is not compromised by anything other than your own fear. This power exists beyond the harm others have inflicted. It exists beyond anything you have experienced. This power comes from your core Self, that part of you that is as it was created and exists untouched by external circumstances. And that Self and its power are to be trusted when you are ready to make the attempt to trust.

Trust yourself and your inner power, for it shall lead you to benefit and abundance.

LOVE AND JOY

You are abundantly loved. You are abundantly worthy of being treated with love and kindness.

Some of you will read those words and reject them, for it is not your experience. However, I assert that it is true. Even if you have not received the love of which you are so worthy, still you are worthy of it. Even if you deny the love of your guides, of the Creative Power, of other humans, still it is there for you when you are able to accept it.

Each of you is created with the capacity to give and receive abundantly. At the soul level, each of you does so. The shift to denial, to rejection, to hoarding your emotions and resources, comes upon incarnation, as does the choice some make to cause harm to others.

All beings are created with free will. The other qualities and capacities with which you are created are subject to that will. Although you may hold within you abundant love, you have a choice of whether to express that love, share it, or keep it to yourself. Likewise, although you are worthy of receiving abundant love, you may choose to reject it or deny it.

It is our hope that you will choose to open to the possibility of giving and receiving love. It is our hope that you will become aware of your core self, the Self that is abundantly deserving of all good things, and that you will accept that this Self is who you truly are.

You are an integral part of the world.

You are abundantly deserving of not only existence, but life. Of joy, love, and compassion.

Some of you read these words and reject them, for this has not been your experience or is not your belief. Yet I tell you that these words are true.

Experiences in your life have left your true Self obscured by the "grime," as it were, of actions and words. For some of you, harm and pain began before you had fully formed your concept of your core Self, and so you became identified with the harm and pain rather than with who you truly are.

You are not those experiences, beloveds. You are not what others have done to you.

You are an integral part of this world, and you are deserving of love, joy, and all good things. You are deserving of fully living a life in which you are engaged, rather than merely existing.

Recognizing and believing these things, living this life, may not be easy. You may have need of aid and support; these are available to you, and there is no shame or weakness in seeking them. Yet it is work which will greatly benefit you should you choose to undertake it.

Today, as every day, you are called upon to work to feel love for yourself.

For some of you, the concept of loving yourself is foreign. You do not believe yourself worthy of love from any. You have suffered experiences for which you blame yourself and believe therefore that you cannot love yourself, for how can you love one who has caused this pain?

Past experiences do not create who you are. They do not define your true self. However, they do cause alterations in how you view yourself and what you feel about yourself. This is why I do not state that you must love yourself, but rather encourage you to take small steps toward doing so. Consider yourself and the qualities you hold which you would admire in others. See whether you are able to love those qualities within yourself.

Healing is not a sudden change, but rather a gradual process of learning to view yourself and your experiences through a different lens. Progressing through this process includes progressing in your ability to love more and more aspects of yourself, no matter how small they may seem, until you are able to feel love for yourself as a whole. This will take time, but you are not alone in the work; those others who love you are with you through the journey.

I ask you, toward whom do you feel love? Is your focus on love of others? On receiving love from others?

Or is your focus on loving yourself?

You can love others without loving yourself, but it is more difficult to receive love from others if you believe you are unworthy of it. How, then, can you give to yourself the love you share with others? How can you gift yourself with this abundant, healing power? For that is what love is at its core: An infinite supply of power which heals and brings growth.

Will you deny yourself this power? Or will you allow yourself to give and receive?

Some state the phrase "Love yourself" as if it were as easy to do as to say. And for them, perhaps it is.

For others, it is difficult. You have experienced harm and abuse at the hands of those meant to cherish and protect you. You have lived within a body that feels unsafe, that has been damaged; or perhaps within a body that is wrong for who you truly are. You have been blamed for what has occurred to you and doubted by those you have trusted with how you feel.

All of these things render the concept of loving yourself foreign and difficult to you. Yet even though some state it as a platitude and put no thought into what it means, still it is one of the truest phrases uttered by humans.

Love is one of the constants in the Universe. All beings feel it, and all beings are worthy of it. You are included in this.

I will not tell you simply to love yourself, for I recognize the difficulty for some of you. I will, rather, say that you are loved, and that you are deserving to receive the same love from yourself that you give to others. And it is my hope that you will begin to feel love for yourself.

In what do you find joy? Or is joy something you believe you are unable to find?

For some, joy is a fleeting thing. For others, due to harm you've experienced or due to illnesses within your mind and body, joy is something you believe you do not feel and perhaps cannot comprehend.

Joy, at its most basic, is simply a sense that love and beauty exist in the Universe as a whole and within your own small sliver of it. It is a sense that you are part of that Whole and that as part of it, you are loved. It is a feeling difficult to describe in human language, but when you feel it, when your heart rises and the clouds lift from your view to show the light, you know what it is.

I encourage you to take time to find one thing, no matter how small, that brings this sense to you. One thing that demonstrates to you the love and beauty within and around you. Consider this thing and fully immerse yourself in the feeling it brings to you.

This is joy. And joy is something of which you are abundantly deserving. I encourage you to allow it into your life and accept it when it comes.

Joy is a fleeting thing for some of you. At times, it passes so quickly you were unaware it was there at all.

Joy can become constant for you if you are open to allowing it into your life. If you are open to seeing what is around you. To feeling as if you are part of the Whole of the Universe.

For some of you, joy is fleeting or appears nonexistent because of illness within you or because of experiences you have had at the hands of others. You cannot simply wish these factors away, and I do not intend to minimize their impact. Simply being open and wanting joy is not sufficient to overcome illness or harm, despite some saying it is so.

However, at times when your mind allows, open to the beauty that surrounds you. Examine what you feel when you observe the sun, or the rain, or other aspects of nature. Notice the emotions when you watch animals or children play or when you are with someone you love.

Joy exists. Experiencing it may be difficult for you, but even if you feel you are undeserving of it, it is there. And you are deserving.

It is my hope that in time, you shall see this and you shall see joy.

UNIQUE, NOT SUPERIOR

It is the nature of humans to have certain perceptions and preconceptions. At times, these are useful in navigating your world. At other times, however, they cause rifts and friction between you and others.

You are not better than any other. While differences exist, these differences do not place any being above another. They merely mean that you are not the same. And this is as it need be, for if all beings were the same, the Universe would not be the glorious tapestry it was created to be.

Even those among you who believe you lack prejudice and preconceptions carry these. Perhaps at a less intrusive level; perhaps you are unaware of their existence. Yet if you are human, these things dwell within your mind.

Examine your beliefs and preconceptions. Examine the visceral reactions within you to those who are different.

This is not judgment upon you. You are human, and therefore will behave and think as a human does. This is simply an invitation to examine the deeper beliefs you hold which may negatively impact you and others. It is an invitation to see all others as equal to you, regardless of who they are, how they appear, or how they live their lives, provided they bring no harm to any through that living.

Difference does not equate to being lesser or better. It equates solely to being different.

No human, indeed, no being at all, speaks for the Creator. We may speak words we believe come from the Creator, or may even speak words which come directly from the Creator. But we cannot speak *for* the Ultimate Creative Power of the Universe, for none of us is that being.

For those who speak directly with the Creator, sharing those words is not the same as speaking *for* that being. It is, rather, similar to relaying a message. The Creator speaks for themself; you simply pass along what it has said.

Some of you have the ability to speak with the Creator or with higher beings who dwell in proximity to the Creator. Indeed, were this ability not to exist, you would not be reading these words, for this is a skill possessed by my host, the person who has typed these words for you to read. Many more of you are awakening to or being trained in this skill.

Be mindful, as you relay the messages you hear and share the wisdom you are given, of representing yourself as one who speaks for the Creator or other beings, rather than one who speaks *with* them. The first positions you in a place of unearned superiority; the second is the truth of the connection and sets you with, rather than above, those who will most benefit from the messages you share.

You are not superior or better. You possess beneficial skills not possessed by all, just as some possess skills in the arts or sciences or other things. Skill is not superiority and does not grant you the right to represent yourself falsely.

I speak to you as what some humans call a "being of light." I speak from a perspective humans cannot have, for you exist on a physical plane while I exist in a dimension of energy and light. You exist within a physical world in which some beings have distanced themselves from the Ultimate Creator, and I speak from a plane close to that Creator.

Yet I am not "better" than you. I am not "superior" to you. I am merely a being whose energetic vibration is higher and who dwells in a different plane in which I have access to broader perspectives.

I am not superior. I am different.

Among humans, there is a tendency to claim or grant superiority based upon certain traits or skills, and to look down upon or shun those who do not possess those traits or skills. This does not make those who claim to be superior any better or more enlightened than the others; rather, the opposite is true. If your "superiority" is dependent upon looking at others as being "lower" or "less than," you are not superior.

We, your guides and beings who work with humans, do not consider ourselves to be better than or superior to you. We are different and, as such, possess knowledge and perspectives we wish to share. We do not come to you as "better," but as collaborators on an equal footing.

We encourage you to see your fellow humans in a similar way. Not as "better" or "lesser," but simply as different but equal.

Examining your deep-seated beliefs and preconceptions is not easy work. Yet it is what you are being called upon to do at this time.

If you are human, and presumably that is the case if you are reading these words, you carry within your mind certain prejudgments and beliefs about others. These may not even be conscious within you, but are the result of what you were taught and what you experienced as a child.

For your world to progress, for peace to exist, for you to be the lightworker or to walk in light as you wish to do, it is time to look within yourself for the roots of prejudice and hatred that grow in the darkness of your mind.

Within you, darkness and light coexist. Within you, certain beliefs exist. This does not render you “a bad person,” merely human. Darkness and light must coexist in balance. However, when you do not look within your own darkness, when you deny it, you are altering the balance in favor of that darkness. What is not acknowledged thrives and grows.

Rather than casting about blame and fault toward others, look first within yourself. What do you believe that is harmful to others? What prejudgments and prejudices do you carry, of which you may not even be fully aware?

Seek to understand these things within yourself. Seek their roots, and then seek and work to remove them. This is part of the work of healing yourself and of healing the world. It is time to begin--or to continue, for some of you have already begun--this work, so that your world may heal and be a more beneficial place for all those who dwell there.

Be mindful of heeding the words of those who seek to convince you that you are somehow better or more enlightened than others because of your spiritual beliefs or practices.

Be mindful, also, of heeding the words of those who seek to convince you that you are worse or less enlightened than they because of their spiritual beliefs and practices.

Beings are different. Beliefs are different. However, existence is not a hierarchy, and having powerful spiritual beliefs does not render anyone superior to any other.

Measure yourself as you are now against who you were in your past, and against who you wish to become. Become the person you wish to be, rather than seeking to become "better" or "more spiritually advanced" than others.

Comparison is the purview of ego, not of the Self. Ego seeks superiority and accolades, while the Self simply seeks to exist in a way which brings benefit. Therefore, you are best served by learning who you truly are, rather than seeking to prove to others that you are superior and somehow more deserving than those who do not share your beliefs and perceptions.

Sharing with others what you know is not wrong. You hold knowledge which may bring benefit to others.

However, be mindful of the ego's tendency to wish celebrity and praise for the knowledge you share. Be mindful of your reasons for sharing.

Some of you chose, when you undertook your current incarnation, to become leaders, yet when you demand and coerce others into following you, that is not leadership.

One does not become a true leader by being the loudest or by insisting that others follow. One becomes a leader by following a path they know to be their own true way, and living a life which encourages others to follow their own paths as well.

The ego will insist that "leadership" equates to having many followers and receiving much recognition and accolades. The ego is incorrect.

Lead through the example of living the life you know to be your true path. Through allowing others to see how you choose to live and how you choose to bring benefit to the world. Live this life for your own sake, not for the sake of what others may say about you or the financial reward it may bring you. When you choose to lead by living your true life, and choose to live this life for your own sake, you may gain what you seek, but this gain is not the purpose of living your life. Your life is intended as a path to your own learning and growth. Whatever you bring into your life as a result of following that path is a bonus, not the core purpose.

When you live in a way such that you seek recognition and praise from others, you are not living as your authentic Self. You are, rather, living from a place of ego and fear.

Ego tells you that you must be recognized. That others must hear and heed your words, for you are "right."

Fear tells you that if you are not recognized, you are nothing. You do not matter.

Both of these are incorrect.

You are not in this life to be lauded and celebrated. You are in this life to bring your unique gifts and perceptions into the world. These gifts and perceptions may never be seen or heard by others, or they may be seen or heard by billions. The size of your audience does not measure your worth, for gathering followers is not your purpose here.

You have come to this world to live a life through which *you* may learn and grow. Through which *you* may become a being of wisdom and understanding. Not to foist this wisdom upon others, but for your own spiritual growth. Sharing with others and bringing benefit to them is merely, as you might say, a bonus.

Live your life to be who you are, and to learn more about who that is. If others benefit from your living and choose to acknowledge that, that is their choice, but let it not be the purpose of your life. Let your purpose be living as your true, core self, for that is where benefit lies.

In your life, you may have learned that pride is a negative quality. This is not necessarily the case.

If your pride crosses into arrogance, into statements that imply you are better than others or into a belief that you are better, this is negative.

However, pride which manifests as belief that you have done well, as a sense of accomplishment and joy in what you have done and who you have become, is a positive trait, for it is acknowledgment of your ability to progress and create.

Therefore, I invite you to take pride in what you have accomplished. To feel joy and love for yourself as you examine the progress you have made in your life. Look back to where you have been, and see where you now stand in your life's journey and your healing journey, and take pride that you have come this far.

You may have further to go, but for today, see the progress you have already made, and be proud of yourself for this.

You are valid exactly as you are. Your existence is valid. Your struggles, your fears, your triumphs, your joys--all these things are valid.

Many times, humans seek to invalidate one another. This may be done on a small scale, such as in cases of bullying or what you call gaslighting. It may be done on a larger, even global, scale, as in cases of discrimination and bigotry against certain categories of people.

This invalidation does not truly render you invalid, for all who exist are valid as they are. But this invalidation does cause harm, both to you and to those who are seeking to create invalidation, for they are harming themselves through their hatred. They are creating a state in which their energetic vibration is consistently low and in which they constantly feel anger, hatred, and a general sense of unwellness that runs deep within them.

All beings are valid as they are. The words and actions of others cannot truly invalidate you, though they may cause you to feel invalid. Know that you are valid as you are, that you are loved throughout the Universe precisely as you are, and that none can change this.

Some humans choose to dislike or even hate those whom they do not understand. They set their beliefs in stone and condemn those who do not follow those beliefs.

This is not a flaw in the targets of that hatred and condemnation. It is a result of fear within those who experience the hatred and express the condemnation.

It is often the nature of humans to fear what you do not understand, and it is, further, the nature of humans to fight and lash out against that which you fear. This is the root of many harmful words and behaviors. When one bullies or abuses another, or speaks words of prejudice and hatred, it is often due to their own fear. They believe, consciously or not, that they must destroy that which they fear so they may reassert their power.

This, of course, does not bring them power. It does not bring them safety or bring an end to their fear. Rather, it perpetuates that fear. It perpetuates their belief they are powerless. And so they continue.

Fear is a human emotion. It is one all of you experience at one time or another. Some of you choose to embrace that fear and use it to build your understanding and your ability to cope with that which rouses your fear. Sadly, others choose to use it to destroy.

How shall you address your fears? How shall you speak to or about the source of those fears? Will you attempt to build understanding within yourself or to destroy that which you fear?

I encourage you to seek and build understanding, for this will heal you and your world.

HEALING IS A JOURNEY

Healing is a journey. At times, it is a long one, one on which you feel isolated and without support.

Know that as you make this journey, you are not alone. Others who are on their journeys likewise feel alone, but collectively, you are many.

Those who are on their own healing journeys do not lose anything by your need for support. There is no time when love and assistance run dry, as it were.

Some of you hold back from seeking assistance on your journeys because you believe somehow that you are taking away support from others. Know that this is not so.

Seek the help and support you need. There is no shame in needing to heal. There is no wrongness in needing support.

You are worthy of being whole, beloveds, for in truth you have always been whole. Parts of you have been harmed, but that does not change you at your core.

Seek the aid you require to reconnect with your core Self and make the journey, for this will benefit you greatly.

Your healing journey is your own. No other may tell you how to accomplish it.

I have stated this in the past, yet many still believe they have the right to tell others how to heal from pain and harm. Many times, this is because they have been on their own healing journey and believe their way is the right way.

Your way of healing is right for you. However, it may not be right for all.

As you progress on your healing journey, know that others may come to you and state that you are doing it “wrong.” That you must engage in certain activities, or believe certain things, or claim blame for what occurred. They may tell you that you are taking too long or that you are not taking long enough.

You may release their words, for they are not you, and your way of healing is valid provided it brings you benefit and harms no one. No one may tell you how you must heal, for your journey is yours and may proceed in the way that works for you.

You are not alone in this journey. Your guides are with you, ready to support you if asked. Other humans are available to support you, if you are able to reach out to them and trust them.

You are not alone, but the journey you undertake is solely yours to form and follow.

No journey is entirely straightforward. The journey toward healing and creating a beneficial life for yourself is no different.

Similarly, no journey undertaken by more than one person is the same for each individual. Your healing journey will not be the same as another's even if your experiences were similar, for you are different people.

Some of you may have been told that your experiences were "not as bad" as those of others, or that you "should be over it" because your experiences have been minimized. Your experiences are your own. The effects of them upon you are yours, for they are not affected by what others tell you they "should" be. And how you choose to heal from those experiences, the path you take, is solely and entirely your own.

Your journey will not be a straightforward path. There will be turns and switchbacks and alternate routes. All of this is as it needs be, for you are on a journey, and journeys take time. Allow yourself this time and this understanding.

As your world gains greater understanding of the effects of experiences upon one's psyche, and indeed upon one's very sense of self, the process of healing will become easier.

As the world gains greater understanding of the reality that people who have experienced pain and trauma did not choose those experiences and do not consciously choose how they respond; as the world more fully understands that these responses and effects may linger for a lifetime even if the traumatic experiences have ended; healing will become more effective and will be embraced rather than rejected or ignored by those with no understanding.

I speak to those who have experienced any form of harm and live with the effects of it: You did not cause this. You did not choose it. And you are not beyond help or hope, though at times you feel as if you are.

Your healing journey is yours to choose, both the processes and, in fact, whether or not to undertake the journey at all. You do not follow this journey alone, however. Support from your guides, from other beings, and from other humans is here when you are ready to ask and receive it.

We who work with humans sorrow at what is done to some of you. You are loved, and you deserve to feel and experience love rather than pain.

You are not alone.

Do you believe you do not deserve to heal? That you do not have the right to be well?

Or is it that you believe you cannot heal, or will not know who you are if you are well?

When one embarks upon a healing journey, particularly when one's sense of self has been warped or obscured by harmful experiences, it is a frightening choice and path. You are leaving familiarity, even if it is a familiarity with things you dislike or that continue to harm you, to step into the unknown.

Know that when you choose to step upon the path of this healing journey, you do so with the full love and support of your guides. Many of you also have love and support from humans around you, though you may be unaware of or resistant to this. Whether you choose to receive the love and support, however, it is there for you when you are ready to request and accept it.

Know, too, that as you progress upon your healing journey, at times it will not be easy. At times, it may seem to bring you more pain. But ultimately, it will bring you great benefit as you go and as you grow.

You have within you the power to heal. You have a true core Self that is who you are and who you will uncover as you progress. And you have the love and support of many, both seen and unseen.

Your healing journey is work. Each step you make necessitates conscious recognition of options, and conscious choice between those options.

At times, this journey becomes exhausting. And at those times, it is not only acceptable but advisable to rest.

No journey is accomplished without respite. When you travel, often you will stop, at least for a moment, to rest. So, too, does your healing journey require times of rest. While you may not entirely cease the work, you need not focus constantly upon it to the point of exhaustion. And if you reach that point, rest is needed, for you cannot progress if you are so tired you cannot see the progression before you.

Allow yourself these times of respite. Know that if you take rest, you shall not fall backward. Your journey shall not be undone by your choice to suspend progression upon it for a brief period. You will return to the journey when you have given yourself time to rest.

As you progress in your healing journey, you will encounter obstacles. You will encounter resistance and fear. At times, you will stall or regress. And these occurrences may cause you to doubt your path, and, indeed, to doubt whether you are capable of healing.

This is work, beloveds, and yet it is work of which you are abundantly capable. A life journey, whether that of healing or of others facets of your life, is rarely, if ever, as straightforward as you would wish.

This journey shall be erratic at times. It is not a straight line, nor a single path, but rather a number of paths, each diverging at points of choice and decision.

At times, the path you choose may prove wrong for you; at those times, regression is necessary to return you to the correct path.

Obstacles arise to give you time to consciously choose the next steps. Stalling allows you opportunity to examine where you are and where you have been, and perhaps to have respite for a short time from the journey.

You are not alone upon this journey, though you may be unaware of or resistant to the love and support available to you. Know, however, that love and support are here when you are willing to reach out for it.

Refrain from judging yourself for the route your healing journey takes, no matter how circuitous. It is your journey, and each step you take brings you closer to your true self.

You, and you alone, are in control of how you manage your past and your life. You, and you alone, have the choice of how and whether to address what has occurred in your past, of how to proceed with healing, of how to structure and create the life you wish to live.

This is immense power, yet it is power some of you deny or ignore. And of which some are unaware.

Others may guide you in your journey. They may offer suggestions. Those who are less beneficial to you may even direct you and issue commands. And yet none of these others may create your life or your healing for you.

Seek aid in your journey as you need, for reaching out for assistance is strength. Knowing when you are unable to proceed alone and require support is a sign of strength.

But know that ultimately, your journey is your own, and you have the power to progress upon it.

The past is not something of which to "let go," but rather something to acknowledge.

This does not mean dwelling and wallowing in it, for that does not allow progress. Rather, it means that for some of you, “letting go” has become synonymous with denial and rejection, and this, too, does not allow progress.

Your past does not define you, but it has helped create you. You can change the effects it has had, but pretending your past does not exist serves no one, least of all you.

At times, too, even as you “let go” of your past, it refuses to let go of you. This may look like people from the past who will not leave you alone, or memories of the past that resurface at their own will. This is not a sign that you are not willing to let go or heal. It is the nature of trauma and of memory.

Acknowledge your past. Accept that it occurred and that it has affected you. You need not cling to it nor embrace it, but acknowledging and accepting are part of the path to healing.

Forgiveness, as often discussed, is not required to heal. You need not excuse the actions of others nor accept any apologies they may attempt to make. You need not even accept these others or their actions.

For healing, the path begins with forgiving yourself for the experiences. You are not, and never were, to blame for what others chose to do, and yet you cling to this blame, to identifying yourself as being at fault. This may not be conscious on your part, and yet at times your actions and your thoughts about yourself are guided by this mindset.

An important step--or steps, for this is a process which will continue throughout your healing journey--is to accept *yourself*, both as the person to whom these things happened and as the Self within you. To accept that you are not at fault, that you did not choose these actions.

And, most importantly, to accept that what others have chosen to do to you has not created you. It does not define you. You may choose to free yourself from those bonds, in whatever ways and whatever time you need.

Forgiveness is not something which you must give to those who have harmed you. It is acceptance of who *you* are, for if you reject and deny yourself, how shall you progress toward healing?

Some of you have been told that struggling with your past is a sign of weakness. Indeed, some have been told that this struggle is a sign that you do not wish to be well.

This is untrue. If you are wallowing and choosing to dwell upon your past, that is your choice, and may be a sign that you have not yet chosen to improve your life. However, if your past clings to you despite your best efforts; if you experience memories and effects against your will; this is not weakness. This is not a sign of your level of desire to heal.

Many things are within your control. However, after extreme events and traumas, some of that control is beyond your awareness, and you do not choose how your mind responds as a result.

Those who have survived damaging experiences inflicted upon them by others are not weak. Surviving these experiences requires immense strength. Choosing to proceed with your life, to try to create a positive life, to work toward healing--all of these are signs of strength.

You are strong. And you are loved.

Many of you who have experienced harm and trauma have had times of believing you are alone. That no other has had experiences such as yours. That only you are “broken” or “damaged.”

Know that this is not so. You are not alone.

Know, too, that as you progress toward healing, you are not alone in this work. Your guides are with you always. These beings, though unseen and perhaps unknown to you, have not left you and are waiting to aid you when you are ready.

Other humans exist who can work with you to assist your progress in your healing journey.

You have never been alone, though it has often felt otherwise. Trust now in the presence of love and the presence of those who wish to support you. Trust that you can become who you wish to be.

Tend to your healing. Tend to your health and well-being.

Some in your life may state that you must devote your time and energy to those around you at the cost of yourself. This is false. While it is not advisable to take away from others, it is even less advisable to take away from yourself. Do you not deserve to heal?

You are not removing anything from others if you choose to devote your time and energy to improving your life. You are the ultimate creative power in your life, and it is acceptable to use this power to create benefit for yourself.

If you choose to give your energy to others at the cost of yourself, you cannot truly bring benefit to them, for you must care for yourself in order to be able to care for others. If you are constantly drained and depleted, how can you provide for anyone?

Tend to your healing, and know that you are abundantly deserving of creating a positive life for yourself. You have this power.

Some of you speak of healing the world, or your country, or a situation in your environment.

While this desire is admirable, I encourage you to first turn your attention to healing yourself.

Some of you seek to heal others, whether on an individual or global scale, out of a true wish to help and express love. Others of you do so to ignore your own need for healing, or because you deny you have anything left to heal within yourself. Denial of pain and struggle is not healing.

Choosing to use your gifts to bring about healing on a broader scale is not wrong, but if you are not progressing upon your journey to heal from your own experiences, the healing you bring to others will be less effective and may not benefit you or them.

Some humans state, "You cannot heal others until you are healed." This is false, and gives rise to the many who obscure their struggles or deny they need to heal, for they so much wish to heal others that they pretend--or even delude themselves--that they have no inner healing left to do.

A truer statement would be, "You must make continued progress upon your healing journey in order to be effective in helping others heal." For all of you carry gifts which can bring about healing; however, it is most beneficial to use those gifts for your own growth and benefit first.

COMPASSION IS KEY

Be gentle with yourself as you progress on your healing journey. Healing is not as straightforward as you may wish it to be or as some claim. You will progress, yet at times you will feel as if you have fallen back to your starting point or even lower.

Each time you make progress, you go further than before. Each time you fall back, you fall back less far, though it may appear otherwise.

You have grown. You have made incredible changes. You--and other humans around you--may not always be aware of these changes, for some of them are subtle and within you and are not visible to the outer eye. But know that the changes and growth have occurred. You are not the person you were even days or weeks ago.

Each time you consciously choose to walk the healing path rather than remain stagnant, you are healing yourself. Each time you consciously choose to embrace your inner power and confront the things you wish or need to change, you are growing.

Be gentle with yourself--and be proud of yourself, for you are stronger and have made more progress than you know.

When trauma occurs, a part of your Self becomes frozen in that moment. These frozen thought-forms, these child-like consciousnesses, then become the parts of you which you reject or attempt to deny.

Your experiences do not create who you are, but they do form the basis for how you are in the world. By embracing and loving these "children" within you, healing begins and progresses.

No part of you is beyond healing. No part of you is hopeless or unworthy. But to receive all that of which you are abundantly deserving, you first need provide it for yourself. You need to provide these inner children with the love and acceptance they have been denied for so long.

Seek aid in this work, for pain may occur, and memories may arise with which you will need support. Find the help you need. But I encourage you to take up this work, for the benefits will be immeasurable.

When one has experienced harm, it is a common reaction to reject what was harmed. To place blame upon the "past self" which had the experience, or to reject the part that was harmed.

Doing this, however, places an obstacle in the path to healing. It is difficult to heal from an experience you deny, or for which you take blame where none is warranted. It is difficult to progress toward well-being when you reject physical and mental aspects of yourself.

What has been done to you in the past is not your fault. There is no fault; there is no blame. There is only responsibility, and you are not responsible for the choices others have made to cause you harm.

You are not responsible for what others have done to you. They, and they alone, bear full responsibility for their choices.

If another spoke to you of their harmful experiences, would you reject them or deny their right to progress toward healing? If not, why do this to yourself?

I encourage you to work toward accepting those parts of yourself which you have rejected due to the harm they have experienced. To embrace the "past self" which is still suffering under the weight of those events.

You deserve to be well and loved, for you did not cause this harm.

Reach out to the parts of yourself you have rejected. The parts upon which you have placed blame. The parts which have been harmed and need your compassion.

These aspects of yourself, whether physical or emotional, are not separate entities; they are part of you. However, for some of you in your healing journeys, you may benefit from addressing these aspects as if they were separate.

Within you, there are frozen consciousnesses. Children, as it were, trapped at the points in time at which harm was experienced. If you view these children as yourself, it may be easy to reject them and even hate them for what they've experienced. However, should you view them as children separate from you, as children who have come to you for aid and comfort, you may find it easier to accept that they did not cause the harm they experienced, and that they are deserving of your compassion and love.

Your healing journey is your own, and at times it may seem insurmountable. Learning to accept all aspects of yourself, even if it necessitates considering them as separate from yourself for a time, will ease the journey. Whatever you need on this journey, so long as it progresses you toward the healing you so abundantly deserve, is acceptable and beneficial.

What do you require to be kind to yourself?

What do the "children" within you wish? What do they need?

Today, I invite you to be kind to all aspects of yourself. This may mean treating yourself in some way. It may mean simply being quiet.

Indulging in what you need and desire is not wrong when it is within your means to provide. Being kind to yourself does not cause struggle, but rather aids in the journey to heal from your past.

Today, be kind. Be, even, indulgent in something which brings you joy.

At times, it is necessary for you to release the perceived need to do things, and simply allow yourselves to be.

When you are unwilling to make that choice, at times it is made for you. When illness invades your body, sometimes this is because you have ignored the signs that you need to rest.

This is not to say that you are to blame for illness. You are not. However, the Universe will become more forceful in its messages if the gentler messages are ignored.

Learn to listen to your bodies and to your minds. Learn to recognize the signs that you need to slow, even to stop for a time. Learn to heed these moments and give yourselves that time.

Some of you measure your life by what you have done. By the accolades and honors you have received. By how many others know your name.

Are these things truly who you are? Is your measure truly made by external factors?

Not everyone will have a wide following. Not everyone will be known beyond their own circles of family and friends. But each action you take, each choice you make in the name of bringing benefit to the world, makes an impact, regardless of the number of people upon whom that impact is made.

Release regret, those who have them, over not reaching "enough" or not doing "enough.

You are enough because you exist. And you have made an impact because you live.

When one speaks hurtful or harmful words to you, it may cause you pain and doubt. You may struggle to release what has been said and to release the person who has said it.

There are those who seek to speak harmful words for the sole sake of doing so. It brings them something they interpret as joy to cause others to feel pain. It is their way of entertaining themselves, for they have no other source of pleasure in their lives.

I do not speak of situations in which another is intentionally and repeatedly abusing you through their actions and words. Nor do I speak of times when another flings slurs related to your race, your identity, or other factors against which they carry prejudice and hatred. Abuse and prejudice are more harmful and damaging to a broader range of people than the behavior I address here. I speak rather of times when someone, perhaps someone you know little of or who is a stranger to you, directs insults and negativity toward you in public or through the virtual venues in which you interact with others.

Although their words cause you pain, and this feeling on your part is valid, it benefits you to move on from their words. To move on from them. They cannot truly harm you, even if they hurt you by what they speak. They are not attacking you, but are rather attacking themselves and life in general through you.

I will not tell you to feel compassion for these people, for that is neither necessary nor easy for those who have been hurt. I will, rather, encourage you to understand that it is pain and damage within these people that cause their actions, and nothing about you. And I will remind you that there are others who support you, who love you, and who will refute these harmful words if you turn to them.

You do not deserve to be hurt or harmed. Not by those close to you and not by those whom you do not know. When another chooses these actions, you have not caused or chosen their behavior, and you may, as you are able, release it.

Illness is not a choice. Receiving harm from another is not a choice.

To some extent, all things in your life are subject to choices, but you do not control the actions of others. You do not control your body chemistry or viruses or bacteria.

Some people condemn those with mental illnesses and those who live with post-traumatic stress as "wanting to be ill." There is a tendency, particularly in communities of those who call themselves lightworkers or spiritual practitioners, to claim that those who live with these conditions could be well if they simply chose to be, and that if you are unwell, it is because you do not wish to be.

It is saddening to note that some of the people speaking this rhetoric, themselves, live with these conditions. And yet they have chosen to blame themselves for something beyond their control, and choose to blame others for those things as well.

Illness is not a choice. Receiving harm from others, and the long-term effects of that harm, are not choices.

If you are unable to "shift your thoughts" or "raise your vibration" and suddenly be free of the conditions with which you live, this is not a sign that you are broken or that you are choosing to be unwell. It is, rather, a sign that some things are not as simple as people wish them to believe.

You deserve to be well. You deserve to be respected and accepted even if you are not well. And these things are not your fault or choice.

Harm which has been caused to you did not occur, as some say, to enable you to heal others or to teach you a lesson. When harm is done, it occurs because someone has chosen to cause harm; there is no other reason.

However, the harm which has been caused to you does not render you "broken" or "damaged." Rather, it renders you in need of healing--and once you have progressed upon your own healing journey, it also renders you one who might help others heal.

Your experiences have not created who you are. They have, however, created within you an understanding of the impacts of harm which is done. They have created an understanding of how to support others in their healing journeys as you continue in your own.

You are not required to assist others in their healing. For that matter, you are not required to engage in your own healing, for everything in life is subject to choice. But know that, should you choose a path which includes aiding others along their healing journeys, your perspectives and understanding will benefit many.

Welcome to a turn of the page, so to speak.

It is time to embrace some of the changes which have been occurring in your life and in your world. While not all changes have been beneficial, some have. Even those that have not have led you to a place where you may now choose the next part of your course.

Choose wisely. Resisting or denying change, ignoring what is occurring around you or believing you are "above" it, is the province of ego. It is not reality. You are part of the world, as much as you may wish otherwise, and you are living a human life at this time. Denying this will not bring you ease.

Change is painful, and it is the nature of ego to resist pain or push it away. Recognize when this occurs, and accept the change regardless.

Your life is improving. Be open to allowing it to do so.

Today, allow yourself to examine and truly see the progress you have made.

You are not the person you were a year ago, or a month, or even a day. Each day that you awaken and choose to continue your journey, each day that you make a choice to benefit yourself and others, each day, in fact, that you are in this world, you create yourself anew.

For some of you, examining how far you have come will draw your focus to mistakes and incorrect choices you have made. I encourage you to remember that you are human. No human is able to always make beneficial choices or to live a life in which they make no mistakes. Narrowing your view to only see the negatives you have done invalidates the incredible progress you have made. Know that even when you have chosen actions you now wish you had not, still you have grown, and the benefit you have brought to the world outweighs the errors you have made.

See how far you have come, beloveds, for we, the beings who work with you, see it and marvel at your resiliency and your power. Today, allow yourself to marvel as well.

BALANCE IS VITAL

The world is filled with light and shadow, for balance is the nature of the Universe.

Yet some of you see only the shadow. Some struggle to see light in the world and in yourselves.

You are a creature of light and darkness, for just as balance is the nature of the Universe, so is it the nature of all beings who exist within the Universe.

Darkness is not to be eliminated, but accepted. It is to be worked with in balance with the light, for at times even darkness can illuminate those things within you that necessitate change or alterations in path.

For those who struggle to find light, know that it, too, is there. Your experiences or other factors within you, such as illness, may cause the light to be more difficult for you to see, but yet it is there.

When you are unable to see the light, look to the sun. To the stars and moon. To the sources of what your eyes perceive as light. And know that this light is within you as well, for you shine with the light of a million suns to those who see your Core Self.

Learn to embrace the light and the darkness, for both are needed. Both are part of you, and you deserve to see them both.

You have been told that you must set aside your anger. That you are not permitted to feel certain emotions about your experiences or the people who were involved.

I encourage you, rather than forbidding emotions, to allow yourself to experience them.

The ability to feel emotions is one of the most profound powers given to humans. It is what makes you human. Emotions are part and parcel of who you are.

Feeling an emotion does not mean reacting in a negative way or choosing harmful actions or words. It means allowing the experience to occur and gifting yourself with the compassion to permit yourself to be human.

Emotions are not the enemy. You are not evil or "wrong" for feeling negatively toward experiences and people that have harmed you. But if you forbid yourself to feel and deny yourself that part of human experience, you are furthering the harm.

Allow emotions. Do so in nonharmful ways, but allow the emotions to exist, and embrace yourself as you feel them.

In your struggle against the things which frighten you, the things which you believe impede you, look within. Often, the greatest struggle comes from denying the fears and emotions within you.

There is no harm in being frightened. There is no shame in feeling emotions. Many times you are taught otherwise, but know that any emotions you experience are acceptable. There is no "bad" or "wrong"; there are only human emotions.

Allow yourself to feel, but examine why those feelings arise. Be mindful of how you express and respond to the emotions. Feeling however you feel is acceptable, but there are unacceptable ways of demonstrating those feelings. Be mindful that you are not expressing your emotions in ways which are harmful or unhealthy.

Allow yourself to feel, for rejecting your feelings is a rejection of your Self.

I encourage you to look inward.

When you have conflict with another, or another has caused you pain, it is human nature to lash out and turn attention to what the other has done. However, in any interaction, there is responsibility on all sides.

You are not responsible for another's choices or actions. You are responsible for your own. What actions did you take that contributed to the conflict? What actions might you choose that will aid you in moving forward?

When another has angered you or brought you pain, you may choose to focus upon their actions and words, but this will prolong the anger and may lead you to speak against them in ways that cause further difficulty. Or you may choose to focus upon what you might have said or done differently, if anything, and on how you can release the resentment against the other and move forward.

Anger is not, on its own, an enemy. But when you choose to cling to it at the cost of healing from a situation, it can become one. Look inward for how you might change your situation, rather than solely focusing outward on what others have done.

In this time of shifts and changes within your life and within your world, know that you are not alone.

When darkness enters your life or your vision, you believe you are the only one experiencing it. You may feel as if no one else has had these experiences or understands what you are seeing and feeling.

Others do understand and yet have the same fears that they are the only one.

Change is one of the only two constants in the Universe, and light and darkness both exist. At times one may be stronger than the other, but still both are present. Balance does not always mean that two qualities exist in the same quantity simultaneously, but that both exist and ultimately have an equal impact.

In times when darkness appears to be overwhelming, know that light is still present, and know that you are not alone in feeling and fearing the darkness. In times when light is more prevalent, reach to those who are experiencing the darkness, for they too need to know they are not alone.

All things pass in time. Light and darkness are a cycle, and it is the way of things that sometimes one is more prevalent than the other. Know this to be so, and know that you are not alone as you struggle in times of darkness.

You gain no awards or accolades for sacrificing yourself in order to provide for others. You are unlikely to receive gratitude for negating your needs in order to meet theirs.

In fact, when you choose constantly to negate and ignore your own needs, others see this and will respond in kind. They see that your needs and wants do not matter to you and so choose not to allow your needs to matter to them either. They see that you are constantly willing to put yourself aside to do what they wish, and so they expect this behavior from you and give no thanks for it.

When you choose to meet the needs of others because it is what you truly desire to do, there is no harm in this. But when you do so out of the belief that they are more important than you, that you do not deserve to have your needs met, this does a disservice to you and to them.

Strike a balance in your life between meeting the needs and demands of others and tending to your own needs and desires. This balance will enable you to live more joyfully and aid them more effectively. And it will serve others, for you are establishing an example from which they may learn to care for themselves.

Some among you see others in pain and seek to raise them up. Even through your own pain, you work and wish to alleviate the pain of others.

This is what is truly meant when one speaks of "lightwork." Although the term has become changed over time, and no longer means what it originally may have, the work of light is to raise others up. To shine light upon them and show them that love exists. This is not done by denying the darkness, nor by insisting that someone change or "only think positively," but rather by shining light that warms, that heals, that acts as a beacon amidst darkness created by others.

Each time you speak kindly to another, you are working with light. Each time you see someone who has been shunned by their peers and accept that person into your group, you are working with light. Each time you speak out against hatred and prejudice, you are working with light.

Some of the greatest work of this kind is done by those who, themselves, have experienced the darkness of others. By those who have experienced pain, harm, and rejection. For these are the people who truly understand how it feels to be rejected and harmed, and they seek to alleviate this in others.

Light and darkness do, and must, coexist to maintain the balance of the Universe. The work of light is not to eliminate darkness, but rather to ensure it remains in balance. Each time one reaches out in compassion and love to another, this is contributing to that balance, for your actions in reaching out balance those of the people who caused pain and harm.

The work of healing, the work of creating your most beneficial life, the work of becoming who you wish to be...all of these are valid and valuable courses to take.

Yet do not dismiss the importance of the work of rest.

This seems a contradiction, yet for some of you, allowing yourself to rest requires more effort than the other work combined.

Balance is needed in all things. The work of living a human life is no different. Between resting and working, balance is vital.

YOU HAVE A CHOICE

If you were to grant the most beneficial life to someone you love, how would it appear? What would that life include? What joy and benefits would it contain?

If you are able to answer this, why do you not choose to grant this life to yourself?

For some of you, it may be that you do not believe the life you envision is possible, or do not believe yourself worthy of it. For others, it may be that you do not love yourself and are therefore unwilling to provide this life to yourself.

As you grow, as you heal, your life will change, for change is part of life and of healing. You have the power to determine what those changes shall be and how they will impact you. This power lies within you and may be accessed at any time. Doing so requires only your willingness and your acceptance of yourself as a being of power.

Will you grant this life to yourself? Or will you continue to believe yourself unworthy? The choice is yours.

You have the power to choose the course of your life.

You have the power to choose when and whether to take actions, to work toward healing from your past, to accept or deny others who wish to be in your life.

Each thing in your life is a choice you may make. And each choice you make strengthens your power to make choices.

Refrain from denying this power. I encourage you to refrain from granting this power to others by insisting that they have caused you to make certain choices or that they have chosen for you. While your choices have been impacted by others' actions or words, still they are ultimately your own.

Accept the responsibility for the choices you have made, and grant yourself compassion for choices which were not beneficial or positive. Accept the power you have to make choices in your life. And accept that you need not allow others to control those choices any longer.

Choice is something often misunderstood. In your lives, many choices are made, and yet often you are unaware that you have made them. At times, you deny even having made a choice, not recognizing that a refusal to choose still is choosing.

You have immense power in your lives, yet many of you have been taught that this power does not exist, and so you choose either not to exercise it or to allow others to take power over you. Again, this is not always a conscious decision, and yet even deciding not to make a choice is still a choice.

Learn to understand the boundaries of your power to choose. Learn to recognize when and where choice exists, and to accept the responsibility for the choices you make.

Each of you has a different path before you. No path is more or less valid than any other, so long as none is harmed by the following of that path. The paths are merely different.

Some of you seek to follow others' paths, and find yourselves unable to do so. You find yourselves uncomfortable or lost. That is because you are not listening to the guidance within you, but rather to what others insist you must do.

Learn to listen to your own inner guidance. Learn to follow one of the paths laid out ahead of *you*, rather than seeking to find your way to a path that has been laid out ahead of another.

There is no "destiny" in the sense of a future set in stone, yet there are paths which are more beneficial to you. Choose from these paths, but know you have a choice. You may, indeed, even choose to follow another's path, but this is unlikely to benefit you, for when you follow another rather than choosing your own path, you are not living in your own authentic way.

Choose your path based upon who you are. Based upon what you know within yourself to be true and to be to your highest benefit. No other being, human or otherwise, can tell you your truth or who you are in your core. Others may assist you in reaching this knowledge, but only you truly know yourself.

You have choices in how you live your life. Although external factors may have an impact, ultimately you are responsible for your life and the decisions you make about it.

It is a human trait at times to deny this responsibility. To state that you are unable to accomplish certain things owing to how others have treated you or behave around you. To state that you have not been given opportunities or skills others possess.

There are effects caused by factors outside yourself, and at times these factors and their effects are beyond your control. This is a truth. However, it is also a truth that you do have control over many aspects of your life.

Focus upon the aspects which are within your control. Focus upon the choices you have available to make. Focus upon what you wish to accomplish and create in your life, and know that you have the power to bring these things into being. If factors outside your control interfere with what you wish to create, you may find other ways to create those things, but choose to take the responsibility that is yours to take.

At times, the choices you make in your life are affected by choices others have made. You act in ways which were exhibited to you in the past, ways which may have brought you pain or harm.

This is not a judgment, for certain actions and choices are imprinted upon you by choices made by others. You learn what you live, so to speak, and when you have lived in pain and fear, it is this which may drive your decisions.

I encourage you to release judgment of yourself for any pain or harm you have caused. Yet know that releasing judgment does not equate to releasing responsibility. If you have caused pain or harm to others through your actions, seek to acknowledge, to yourself and to those others where possible, your responsibility. To apologize and make amends if this is within your ability.

Know, too, that going forward you may take control of your actions. You may learn to recognize when you are embarking upon a course of action, when you are making choices, which are based upon what others have done to you in the past. You may learn to make alternate choices.

It is within your power to correct your course. I encourage you to embrace this power, for you need not continue to live imprisoned by what has occurred in your past.

You are under no obligation to maintain connections with any other human.

Often, it is said that you must keep ties with another because they are related to you, or because you work with them, or for any number of other reasons. This is not the case. If a connection with another causes you pain, or if it is a situation that brings toxicity or harm into your life, you need not maintain that connection.

Some connections are easier to sever than others, but you do not owe anyone a place in your life, regardless of who they are.

Form connections that bring you peace. Connections with those with whom there is mutual respect and support. And remove the connections that bring you difficulty and pain.

This is not a command but a choice you may make, for your life is your own, and the choice of who is part of that life is also your own.

Among you, there are those who say that any negative experience you have had, no matter how damaging, was necessary for your growth and learning.

We, your guides and other beings who work with you, wish you to know that this is inaccurate.

You do not choose to be harmed. Not in your current incarnation and not on the level of a soul between incarnations. Nor do you exist to help others learn their lessons and progress in their growth.

When harm is caused to you, it is something which occurs on the physical plane, the plane in which you exist. It is something which is chosen by the perpetrator of the act, not by the one who is harmed.

You may choose to learn and grow from your experiences. This is a beneficial choice you may make, for it is possible to find growth and progress in any experience you have. But this was not the "intended purpose" of those experiences. This was not a "lesson you chose to learn."

It is an unfortunate truth that at times, one causes harm to another. Know that any harm that has been caused to you was not due to a "soul contract" or to any choice you made, whether consciously or not. It was due solely to the choices of the one who caused harm. And you may make the choice to disassociate yourself from their choices and actions and choose to heal from what has occurred.

No one, in looking back at their life, is pleased or proud of every choice they have made. As you have the power to choose, so you have the power to choose incorrectly, to choose actions or words which are not beneficial or even are harmful to you or to others.

These choices were unwise, but they do not render you a "bad person." Humans make choices in response to other factors, at times. In response to their own experiences, or to incorrect beliefs they have been taught.

Choosing poorly does not mean you are not a good person. It means merely that you have at times made poor choices. Part of the healing journey upon which you have embarked necessitates accepting yourself and granting yourself compassion for and despite these choices.

You are on a journey. You are learning and growing, and as you do so, your choices will improve and be more beneficial. Meanwhile, honor who you were that made the unwise choices, and know you have the power to choose more wisely now and in future.

No one else can create you. No one else can choose what your life becomes. These are choices that are entirely within your power and purview.

At times you feel as if you are the sum of what others have done to you, said to you, and think about you. You feel as if you must create your life based upon what others believe you to be and what they expect you to do.

This is an abdication of the power inherent in your existence. Why do you choose to deny yourself use of the power with which each being is imbued?

For many of you, this is not a choice you have made consciously, but one sparked by your past experiences and by lessons others have taught you. You have been conditioned to believe yourself powerless, to believe that life simply happens to you and is beyond your control.

While there are facets of your existence which are indeed beyond your power, such as the actions of others, there are many things to which your power extends if you are willing to accept it.

You alone have the power to create the life you wish to live. In your core, your true Self knows this to be true and is awaiting your decision to embrace and use this power. When shall you make this choice?

For some of you, accepting your power to make choices for your life is difficult. You have become invested in holding others responsible for your decisions, or have become identified with being one to whom things happen rather than one who causes things to happen.

It is time to release these perceptions, for they are false. Others may have committed actions which influenced your decisions, but ultimately the decisions were yours. Things have happened to you, and at times these things were beyond your control, but you do possess the power to cause things to happen for you rather than waiting for things to occur.

As you learn to accept and embrace this power, as you learn to recognize your role in creating your life, you will find abundance and joy, for you will learn to create those things. You will learn that they are within your power, for you are deserving of them and can have them if you choose.

Choose wisely. Choose well.

CHANGE IS CONSTANT

Many shifts and changes await you. Many have already occurred.

You resist change in the world as a whole, for the thought of living in a world that is different frightens you. This fear of change is understandable.

Yet you also fear change within you. You fear that you will not recognize yourself. That you will become someone new.

Of course you shall become someone new, beloveds, for each time you make even the tiniest of changes, you are creating yourself anew. You are not meant to live a life of stagnation and sameness. For you to fully embrace life, change must occur.

You are not alone in your fear, nor are you alone as you accept and allow the changes. You are supported by your guides, by other beings, and by humans who care for you. Some, perhaps, whom you have yet to meet, and yet their care shall reach you across time when you are ready to accept.

Be who you are guided to be. Become the person who shall reach the next stage of your life. I do not tell you to release fear, for some of you find this impossible. Rather, I tell you to allow fear but to also allow the change, for as you progress, the fear will lessen.

Where you are now in your life is acceptable and valid.

Where you wish to be in your life is acceptable and valid.

You are not lessened by your experiences, nor by any difficulties which arise as a result of those experiences.

You are not "less than" others who have not had similar experiences, or than those who have progressed further in their healing journeys than you have in yours.

You are you, beloveds. Abundantly loved, though you may not see or accept this love. Abundantly deserving of healing, of creating a life in which you feel heard and accepted.

You may create this life. You may choose not to. You may reach out for support and assistance, or not. Whatever choices you make as you progress in your life, they are solely yours to make. Wherever you start, and however you grow, it is your choice.

Choose wisely, not based upon what others tell you, but upon who you know yourself to be or wish to become. And you are not alone.

What path shall you choose for the next part of your life?

For many of you, it is a time of change. Of new decisions, or the reconsidering of decisions already made.

Changing your course does not equate to failure or to "giving up." In all lives, for all beings whether human or not, there come times when it is wise to examine the course you have set and determine whether it continues to benefit you.

Change does not mean failure. Choosing to set a new course, to follow a new path, does not mean you have given up. It means you possess the wisdom to know that sometimes, the course upon which you had set out is no longer the most beneficial course to follow.

Recognizing the need for change is not weakness or fear. Clinging to what no longer serves you is caused by fear and ego. Being willing to release those things is wisdom and strength.

It is time to determine your next path. You stand at a crossroads, and the choice is entirely yours to make. What path shall you choose?

Know, as you make this decision, that you are not alone. You are loved and supported. And if you choose something which proves not to benefit you, the choice may always be altered.

What shall you become? Whom shall you be as you accept the changes which occur in your life, as you accept healing and growth?

Whom do you wish to be? What do you wish to become?

Change is not something that must happen to you, but rather something which you bring to bear. You are the force behind the changes which occur in your life. You may choose to embrace that power and work with it to create the changes you most desire, or simply allow things to happen.

Whom do you wish to be? What do you wish to become? You alone have the power to create the life you wish to live, to create yourself as the person you wish to be. None can do this for you, for the power is within each of you. Others may guide you to seeing and accepting this power, but only you have the power to create your life.

Embrace this power, for as you progress in your life, change will occur whether or not you consciously create it. You may choose to create, and I encourage you to make this choice.

Many of you have experienced many shifts and changes over the past year. Some of these changes have been painful. Some have involved loss.

Know that this time has brought you tools and skills for your progression into the next phase of your life. Know, too, that the sadness and grief this time has brought you are not negated, for those emotions are valid. Your means of dealing with them are valid so long as they bring no harm to yourself or others.

Some of the struggles are now reaching their end. You have choices ahead of you about how you wish to proceed in your life.

As you make your choices, you are not alone. Your guides and those who love you are with you.

Use the tools you have gained to guide the next leg of your journey, and know that should you choose incorrectly, you always have the option to change your course.

In such a short time, so much has changed in your lives. Some of you look back across the months and cannot conceive of everything that has vanished or been lost. Some can barely remember the time before the current restrictions and regulations in your world.

Know that change is constant, but more importantly, know that regardless of how rapid the changes occur and how overwhelming they appear, you do not face them alone. Each of you is supported by your guides, by your loved ones, by other beings who are with you even if you are unaware.

Your world shall continue to change, for change does not cease. As long as life itself exists, so too shall change. But know that you do not face it without love and support. You are held.

Growth is frightening to some of you. Change is terrifying. Yet you know that life is about growth and change.

Being frightened is acceptable. However you feel is acceptable. When you have lived a life full of pain, you fear many things.

Yet you can act despite the fear. You can grow and change even when it feels too much, too frightening, too overwhelming. You need not let the experiences of your past and the fear arising from them prevent you from growing into the life you truly wish to live.

I will not tell you to release the fear, as for some of you this act is not as simple as it sounds. I tell you, rather, to act in spite of the fear. To know that you are not alone and that you are abundantly able to do all that you wish to do, when you choose to cease allowing fear to choose for you.

This is not easy work. You may require help and support to accomplish it, and that is wise and is valid. But you can do it.

At times, change in your life occurs at what you may call a whirlwind pace. It seems as if things happen so quickly you cannot comprehend them, nor can you adjust to one change before another occurs.

Seize hold of the changes as they occur. Rather than resisting change, allow it, but do so in a way that acknowledges the power within you that has created it. For any change which occurs in your life is due to your own creative power.

You do not create harm done to you, for this is created by those causing the harm. But you create your healing path when you are ready to heal. You create the benefits which come to you. You create the meeting of those who might aid you in your journey.

Change is a constant. No being can resist change entirely, for change will occur whether it is consciously desired or not. By learning to consciously desire and embrace it, and to live within it as it occurs rather than rejecting it, you shall find it less overwhelming and it shall more likely lead to the creations you wish to have in your life.

The power for change is within you. The power to create your life is also within. Embrace this power, for it is an intrinsic part of you and will bring great benefit if you allow it to do so.

Resisting change does not prevent it. It prevents only your ability to cope with it. Your ability to embrace it and guide it in the direction you wish to go.

However, attempting to force change does not cause it, or may not cause the change you wish. The more you push and force, the more resistance you will encounter, until things grind to a halt or change occurs in a way not beneficial to you.

Learn to accept change, for it is one of only two constants in the Universe. The other constant is love, and I encourage you to learn to love change and love what it brings to you. At times change is negative and harmful to you, and this need not be loved, but it must be accepted, for it will occur regardless.

Many times, though, positive change is overlooked or not seen because you resist either through fear of change or through effort to bring about a different change. In these times, look to what the change brings you and attempt to feel love for the positives.

Change will occur. When you accept the changes and allow them, your life will become more positive and will flow more easily toward the abundance and benefit you desire.

You are abundantly deserving of love and joy. Having these in your life detracts from no one, for these qualities are among the most infinitely available in the Universe.

Yet some of you do not realize that you are so deserving, or are unable to believe it. Some of you fear gaining love and joy because you believe you will take away from others. Some of you fear gaining it because of what you might lose. An existence in which happiness and love are lacking feels familiar to you even if you dislike it, and you are unwilling or afraid to lose that familiarity. You are unwilling or afraid to lose the people in your life who benefit from your willingness to place their desires above your needs.

You are not present in the world solely to fulfill the needs and wishes of others. You bring them no joy when you capitulate to their every request or demand, though at times you do so in an attempt to bring them joy. You do yourself no service by constantly placing yourself at the service of others while ignoring your own needs.

You are abundantly deserving of love and joy. Is it not time to allow yourself to have these things?

Is your life lived according to what you need and desire? Or have you constructed a life based upon what others tell you or what you believe they want from you?

In coexisting with others, of course they must be considered at times. Ignoring the needs of others or deliberately choosing actions which you know may negatively affect them is not beneficial to anyone. However, if you are sacrificing your true self in order to appease others, you are not living the life you are meant to live.

No one in this world is so important that you must subjugate yourself and pretend to be someone else in order to please them. If someone in your life does not accept you as you are, perhaps they do not truly have a place in your life, for those whom you allow close to you need only be there if they are willing to accept your true self.

I encourage you to begin now to craft a life in which you are authentic and true to who you are inside. In which you remove the mask you wear to soothe others' feelings and opinions, and instead show the brilliant light that hides beneath that mask. Some may refuse to accept you, but this is a reflection upon them, not you. Others will be drawn to you, for when you show who you truly are, you become a beacon for those who belong in your life.

You deserve to be seen for who you are.

Why do you doubt yourself? Your skills, your knowledge, your intuition. Often, you choose to reject these things and instead believe others hold more knowledge and wisdom than you.

You have within you abundant wisdom and understanding. You alone see the world as you do, for no two humans see things alike. The world, indeed, the Universe, needs your unique perspectives and perception, for without each being, a piece is missing.

Trust what you hold within you. It may be obscured by past experiences and traumas, but it is there. Learn, seeking aid if needed, to reach past the damage and residue of your past to connect with your true Self, your true core, and trust what is there.

For some of you, this work will be difficult and even frightening, for you have come to know yourself as the sum of your experiences and the effects those experiences have left. Know that you do not undertake it alone; if you are able to ask for support and assistance, whether from your guides or from humans, it is here for you.

Release your perceived need to allow others to tell you how to live, how to be, how the world is. Instead, embrace your own inner knowing and its validity. You are abundantly wise. You have merely forgotten what you know.

In your past, you have lived a life in which being your authentic self was undesirable and perhaps unsafe. You have learned to hide. You have learned to construct a facade to cover your truth, and at times doing so was a matter of survival.

If you are still in a place where it is unsafe to be who you are, I encourage you to seek assistance in leaving that situation. You deserve safety and kindness. There are those who will help you in achieving it if you are willing to reach out.

However, many of you are no longer in unsafe situations, yet you continue to live a life in which you seek safety at the cost of truth. You fear others will not accept you should they learn who you truly are, so you maintain the facade and the perceived safety even though it becomes painful for you to continue to hide.

Beloveds, you need hide no longer. It is true that some will refuse to accept who you truly are, but this is not your responsibility. Some cannot see beyond the beliefs they hold within them, and some will struggle to accept the "changes" you make because they will not understand that you are changing into who you have been all along. Or perhaps because they cannot see beyond themselves and will take your changes personally. Again, this is not your responsibility.

No matter who is in your life, even if you are parenting young children for whom you are responsible, your first responsibility is to yourself. This does not mean to ignore responsibilities to others, but rather that you cannot effectively meet your responsibility to others if you ignore your own needs. If you ignore your own truth.

It is time to uncover that truth. It is my hope you will begin.

Some of you are called now to close a chapter of your lives and open another. This is work which feels frightening to you. Some do not see how it is possible to follow the course you see before you. Others fear the reactions of those in their lives who are impacted by the change and even of those who are not relevant to their lives.

Know that if you feel this call, it is time to act. Resisting will lead only to more struggle and pain as you refuse to acknowledge the course you know is right for you. This call comes from within you but also from the Universe and from your guides, and ignoring it may lead to greater efforts to bring you to attend to the call. These efforts may leave you no options.

You are not asked to ignore or deny your fear. You are, rather, asked to act despite it. To reach out for support through the fear but to progress regardless. Fear is a human emotion, and you are not called on to deny any emotions, but rather to respond to them in ways that do not cause harm to any, including yourself.

Denying yourself options which you feel deeply will bring you joy and benefit is a form of harm, for when you deny these options, you condemn yourself to a life in which you feel pain and lack. A life in which you come to resent those upon whom you place the fault for “holding you back” and, worse, come to resent yourself for not making steps toward change.

The next stage of your life journey will not be without difficulty, for any stage of any human life contains some negatives. However, this next stage shall bring you more benefit than your current one when you are willing to step into it.

You carry within you a light which is sorely needed in this world. Yet you fear displaying this light to others. Perhaps you have been condemned in the past for traits others found undesirable, or perhaps you have lived in environments where your truth was unsafe.

The Universe needs what you hold within. Your light, your truth, are needed at this time to bring about changes which will render your world a safer place for others as well as for yourself.

Displaying your true self, shining your light, feels frightening, for it is not something which has been encouraged in your life. Yet the longer you hide, the more painful it becomes for you to pretend to be something you are not.

Allow that light to show. Allow your core Self to bask in the glow of day, for a new day now begins for you if you are willing.

CONSCIOUS CREATION

You may have heard others speak of "conscious creation." Those others may have taught, or you may have erroneously believed, that creating consciously requires pushing your creative power in specific directions. That it requires you to be in full control and force the creations your conscious mind conceptualizes.

This is incorrect.

To create consciously, one must be conscious of wielding the creative power, but one must also be mindful of thoughts, words, and actions that place obstacles in the power's path. One must be mindful of "trying to create," for what the mind considers, the power will bring to bear--and in "trying," the mind considers that which the person does not want, for you consider the thing you wish to eliminate rather than what you wish to bring to bear.

Conscious creation means awareness of your thoughts and awareness of the creative power as a sentient force that wishes to work with and for you, and the knowledge that your ego fears this power and endeavors to work against it on a subconscious level. When you create consciously, you are conscious of this internal opposition and learn to release it and allow the power to do its work. It means recognition that your conscious mind does not hold all knowledge, including all knowledge of what will truly benefit you.

To create consciously, you are asked to release the effort to create and simply be aware and work with your own internal creative power and the thoughts and emotions within yourself that hold back this power.

All of you have the ability to do this. You need only trust yourselves, though for some, this is more difficult than it seems. And yet you have this ability as well.

You carry within you the power to craft the life you wish to live. You carry the knowledge of what is in your highest benefit. You carry the wisdom and discernment to know whether something will truly benefit you.

Many of you doubt these things. You doubt or refuse your power, because you have been told and shown that you do not possess it or because you fear misusing it. You believe you do not have the knowledge and wisdom, or that others know better and are wiser than you and should therefore be heeded above what you know within yourself.

I encourage you to recognize that these things are truly within you, even if you have become disconnected from them by the actions or words of others. I encourage you to embrace and reclaim your power over your own life and the course upon which you travel.

Your life belongs to you. No other has the right to create it for you or to tell you what you must create. No course is set in stone, and you may alter what you choose should it prove incorrect for you, but this decision, too, rests solely with you.

Claim your power, and trust yourself to use it for your highest ideal. Embrace your knowledge and wisdom, and trust that it will guide you to the most beneficial course.

No other, even your guides, even the Creator, can override your choices unless you allow this to occur. Learn to choose what is truly in your highest benefit and to trust in what you choose.

It is the nature of many humans to put effort into things which do not require it. Some of you have learned through past experiences that you must push, you must exert, you must force your way through life. This is a response to circumstances in which your needs went unmet when you did not push and force, but you are no longer in those circumstances.

You are not faulted for creating greater difficulties for yourselves, for this is a lesson you have been taught. It is a common belief among humans that you must "try harder," even at a cost of physical or emotional health, to achieve.

We, your guides and other beings who work with and observe humans, wish you to know that you need not "try harder." In fact, this effort often holds back that which you most wish to create. Maximum effort creates maximum resistance.

In order to fully embrace your inner power and create the life you wish and deserve, you need to learn to stop exerting so much effort and allow the power to flow. Learn to cease opposing your own power. This power is like a river which flows without needing effort or direction; you constrain it and "dam it up," so to speak, when you attempt to control how it works.

This is not to say that having a goal in mind is wrong. It is wise to know what you wish to create. But it is equally wise to believe that the power within you and around you knows what is to your highest benefit, and when you constrain that power, you block the creations of benefits your conscious mind does not conceive.

Less effort creates greater benefit. Work to exert less effort and allow your power to flow as it will, and know that it will flow to what will most benefit you.

"Go with the flow" is a phrase which humans use with great frequency, yet many are unable to actually do so.

The "flow" is creation. The "flow" is the power that dwells within each of you to heal, to grow, to learn, and to change. Yet your egos fear that power, for "going with the flow" necessitates entering the unknown.

When you resist "the flow," you do not receive benefit. You go on disliking the life in which you live, or railing against certain people and circumstances in that life, and believing you cannot change. And when you attempt to force that power to flow as you consciously want it to, your ego interferes and leads your power to create a continuation of your current circumstances.

I do not speak in cliches and platitudes generally, but for this message, the phrase will suffice more than my usual words. Go with the flow, beloveds, and know that this flow is the creative power within you that shall lead you to the life you truly desire and deserve. Allow this power to flow.

Allow yourself, for one moment, to envision the life you most wish for yourself. Where would you live? With whom would you surround yourself?

Who would you be?

This last question can be frightening for some, for you do not know who you are now, and the thought of who you might become if things change is more than you feel able to manage at this time.

Know that who you are now may be obscured, but you are the person you were created to be. This person may be hidden beneath layers of pain and harm, yet they still exist within you.

The person you would be if you lived the life you most wish is that core person. The person within you, beneath those layers.

You have the power within you to become that person once again. To work to heal from your past, though this is work that will never be completed, for healing is a journey rather than a finite ending. Yet healing is possible.

Know that you, at your core, have never changed from the person you wish to be, and you may find that person again with work, with help and support as needed. You are not alone.

When I speak of the power each being has to create their own life, I do not mean that you choose to create experiences which have harmed you. I do not mean that you somehow created or chose the actions of others that caused you pain.

You carry within you the power to create, yet often are unaware that this power exists, and so do not utilize it. The power you have to create your life informs your own actions and choices when you are aware of how to exercise that power. It does not bring evil or harm into your life; it provides means to bring benefit and love when you are aware of how this power may be used.

Some have twisted the meaning of the statement "you create your reality" into victim-blaming and cruel rhetoric that furthers abuse and harm. This is not the intention of the phrase--or of the creative power you carry within you.

In your healing journey, you may learn to embrace your creative power and use it to bring healing and benefit to your life. This is a choice you may make. But even should you choose not to embrace this power, still you do not create others' negative choices toward you.

You did not create the harm that was done to you. Any who says otherwise is speaking falsely.

What do you most desire to create in your life?

For some of you, there is no easy answer to that question. You struggle to determine what you wish to create, for you have never been granted the freedom to create before. Or you have had it but were unaware.

You have that freedom. All that you desire, all that you need, can be created. It is not an easy task, for much work must be done within yourself to accept your power and to accept that you deserve to have benefit and love and joy in your life.

But it is possible. It is within your grasp.

Start by answering this question: What do you most desire to create? Refrain from judging your response; merely allow your soul to respond.

I ask you this: What, in all the Universe, do you most wish to bring into your life?

You struggle with this question, for you do not believe you are deserving of this. Or perhaps because you have never believed you had the ability to create that which you wish to have in your life. These beliefs may come from within you, but even then, they were most likely established by others.

When you have been mistreated, you do not believe you are worthy of having what you wish. When you have been forced to act purely out of survival, you struggle to conceptualize a life lived upon the basis of what brings you joy and fulfillment rather than what simply allows you to survive.

Some of you are no longer in the place where mere survival was all you could manage and all you knew to do. Yet your minds are still stuck in that place. The frozen consciousnesses within you, the "children," are unable to recognize that you have left that place.

For those who are still in situations in which mere survival requires your full attention and energy, I encourage you to seek aid in leaving that situation and finding safety. This is not treatment of which you are deserving, and it is bringing you harm.

For those who have left those situations, I encourage you now to look around you and realize that you have progressed beyond mere survival. It is time now to move toward and create a life in which you truly live.

Your world awaits you. Your life awaits you.

You have held back from the life you wish to create, perhaps out of fear or out of disbelief that it is possible. You have held back from giving yourself the gift of the abundant life you deserve because you question whether you truly deserve it.

As you hold back from yourself, you hold back also from the world. You keep it at arms' length, or refrain from offering to others the gifts you possess which would benefit them. You refrain from making a difference in the world, perhaps believing that you cannot make a positive difference.

The life you wish to create is there for you. It already exists as one of several potential futures; all that is required to bring it to fruition is your choice to do so. The benefit you may bring to others likewise exists in potential, and you have the power to choose to bring it into reality.

Your world awaits you. Your life awaits you. Perhaps it is time to end the waiting and take the actions to create this reality.

Your power lies in your ability to survive and surpass events which occur in your life. This power has brought you to this place and time, the place and time in which you read these words and live your life.

This power shall lead you further in your life, into a life which you most wish to live. However, for this to come to pass, you must allow it to be so.

Some of you speak of "creative power" as something which you must exert over circumstances and even over other humans in order to form that which you wish to receive. This is an inaccurate belief. The power to create your most beneficial life does not respond to force or exertion. It acts when you allow it. When you open yourself to fully knowing and accepting that you have this power and that it knows what you most need.

You try too hard, beloveds, and this counteracts the power which is available to you. Learn to relax the effort and simply be open to the power and what it brings you. This is the way you shall create what will most benefit you. Your minds may be unable to conceptualize what benefits await you; when you "try" to create, you close doors to benefits you cannot or do not imagine.

Be open to the creative power within you and *allow* it to work for you rather than endeavoring to force it to do so.

CONNECTING WITH THE WORLD

Many times, people are blamed for things which have been done to them. People are told they have chosen to be harmed, that they have a "lesson to learn," or that it is something they have manifested through "low vibration."

None of these things is true.

When one person harms another, it is not the fault or responsibility of the one who was harmed. Each human has free will. Each person chooses their actions. If one chooses to cause harm, that is their choice and therefore their responsibility.

Stating that someone who has been harmed is at fault is, itself, abusive behavior. You are furthering the harm and pain the person has already experienced by informing them they have chosen it.

You are, of course, free to believe what you wish to believe, for free will includes that freedom. However, I encourage you to refrain from telling someone who has trusted you enough to come forward with a story of abuse and harm that they chose it or wanted it, for that does not benefit them and shows you to be as harmful as people in that person's past.

You carry no blame for the experiences others have inflicted upon you. Any harm caused to you by others is their choice and responsibility, although they have claimed otherwise.

You do not choose the actions of others, only your own. You do not create or control what others choose to do; you have power only to create and control your own decisions and actions.

These words will not dissolve the guilt and blame you feel for what has occurred in your past, for that dissolution will take more time and more aid than simply words you read upon an electronic screen. Yet it is my hope that they shall enter your consciousness and begin the process of aiding you in releasing blame for something that has never been your fault.

There is no fault. There is no blame. There is only responsibility, and you are not responsible for what others have done.

Although a corner has been turned in your world, the work of building a more beneficial world has not ended.

Each of you has choices to make as you proceed through your lives. These choices may benefit you. They may benefit others. Or they may benefit no one...for even a negative choice is a choice.

Consider carefully what contribution you wish to make to your own life and to the lives of those around you. These contributions need not be grand and broad, but still the choice is yours.

Your world is changing, and you have a role to play, if you choose to play it.

It is not for you to attempt to change all the difficulties in the world. It is not your role to change the minds of those who disagree with you, or to counteract their statements.

I do not speak of things like prejudice and hatred, nor of things which cause harm, but of disagreements in opinion, or the tendency of each human to have different views and perceptions.

At times, some of you become invested in attempting to force others to see things your way rather than simply accepting that your way is not the only way. This causes conflict and at times causes pain and anger. Nothing is resolved through this, and you merely push others further from seeing your point of view.

Release the need to be right. Release the need for others to agree with your assertions. State your beliefs and opinions, but be mindful also of how you do so, for it serves no one if you are negating others in the pursuit of proving yourself.

In the past year, your world has changed greatly. Your relationships have changed. Your way of acting and interacting has changed.

While the reasons behind these changes were negative, consider this as a benefit: This has shown that you are capable of change. That although change may be painful and unpleasant, you have within you the power to accomplish it.

In the Universe as a whole, there are two primary constants: Change and love.

Some of you embrace both. Some, often owing to past experiences, reject both.

I encourage you to embrace change when it is presented, though it is unnecessary to enjoy or welcome it. Embracing it merely means accepting it and seeking the positive aspects brought by it.

More importantly, I encourage you to embrace love in all forms. Love of your family, whether biological, chosen, or both. Love of your friends. Love of your partners. And above all, love of yourself, for you are as abundantly deserving of love as any.

For some of you, love is more difficult to accept than change. Know that as you open yourself to feeling and receiving love, so too shall change become less difficult.

Engage today with the sunlight. With trees and grass if you are able. With the sky, the air, the earth.

Engage with the world around you, for you are not separate from it. You are, rather, an integral part of it.

Were you not to exist, the world would not be as it is now, for each life upon this Earth, within this world, contributes to it.

You are needed, for without you, the world would not be as it is. And although your world has flaws, and is a world in which some struggle and suffer, it also contains beauty, wonder, joy, and love. These positive qualities would be muted were it not for your contribution.

Engage, then, with the beauty. With the wonder. Allow yourself to experience the joy of connection with the world in which you live. And open yourself to feeling and receiving the abundant love around you.

You are not isolated. You are not alone.

Often, some of you feel as if you are both of those things. That you have no one in your life to offer you love and support; that you have no connection to those amongst whom you dwell.

These feelings are valid, and yet they are an illusion. They are brought about by past experiences, or by the inner workings of your mind. This renders them no less valid, yet it means they are not complete truth.

Always, your guides are with you. Always, the Universe, the elements, other beings in which you believe, are all with you. Even when it seems all other humans have forsaken or rejected you, still you are not alone.

For some of you, your past experiences have left you unable to connect with yourself, let alone others. Connection feels frightening and dangerous. Yet unless you are willing to attempt connection with yourself and, when you are ready, with others, your healing journey will progress slowly and may at times halt.

Allow yourself to feel the connections with the world around you. With nature, with your guides, with other beings, and with the Universe as a whole, for it is from this that you were created, and you are an aspect of it.

You are not alone.

At this time, many of you feel overwhelmed by incidents, events, and circumstances in your own lives and in the world around you. Some of you believe you cannot overcome this sense of stress and fear.

Know that in time, it will pass. No circumstance in a human life endures forever. Even the darkest times end, giving way to light and positive occurrences.

This is not to say that you "should" not fear, for "should" is a word we refrain from using when discussing these things with you. There is no "should." There is wise action and less wise; there is beneficial and detrimental. The choice of which type of action to utilize is entirely your own.

But know that your fears that this difficult time will not pass are untrue. It is your ego attempting to hold you back. It is your inner children feeling the emotions children feel when faced with that which seems overwhelming. It is not your true Core Self; that Self knows that all things pass in the fullness of time, and that just as you have overcome past experiences, so shall you overcome what you experience now.

You are supported and held by those who love you, both seen and unseen. You shall pass through this time and into a time of benefit. Know this to be true.

In any community of humans, there is inclusion and exclusion. It is, unfortunately, human nature to create categories of "us" and "them," and to exclude any who appear to fall into the category of "them."

It is saddening to see this exclusion and categorization occur within communities of people who call themselves spiritual or healers. Excluding others, bullying them, discriminating against them, is the antithesis of healing. It is the opposite of spiritual.

While it is unnecessary, and improbable, for one to like all others, it is equally unnecessary to be cruel to one whom you dislike. Speaking behind them, using cruel words toward them, even wishing them ill because you dislike them or disagree with their stance, is harmful to them and to you.

Bullying and hatred are not spiritual acts. I encourage you to examine how you have treated others within your community and others who have attempted to become part of it. If you speak of "high vibration only," yet also speak hate-filled words toward those who do not agree and act as you believe they should, your own vibration is not as high as you wish to believe.

One of the few constants in the Universe is love, yet some of those who claim to be in connection with the Universe espouse hatred. Be mindful of your thoughts and words. Be what you wish to believe you are.

SHIVA'S CLOSING MESSAGE

I am thankful to have had the opportunity of sharing my perspectives and knowledge with you through this book and its predecessor, as well as through the messages which were previously shared online. It has been an honor to work thusly with you.

I have not left. I have not gone anywhere, and am still working closely with the human you know as River Lightbearer. For some of you, should you choose to seek a session with River, I will be contributing. I also continue to contribute to written materials created by River.

Although I am a being of light, and have little experience in being human, I am pleased to be able to work with humans. Your world is different from the plane in which I exist, yet many similarities appear. In both worlds, light and darkness coexist, as they must in order for the Universe to maintain balance. In both, individual beings have their own understanding and perspectives, and at times may disagree with one another.

You and I are different, but neither is more or less than the other. The information and knowledge I share is not intended as an implication that I am more intelligent than you or that I am an expert in your life and existence. I simply have knowledge to which you may not have access; at the same time, each of you possesses knowledge that I do not.

It is my hope that the words contained in this book will facilitate your growth and your healing journey. I intend them to be words of empowerment and benefit rather than words that lead you to believe you are lesser. You are not less than I. You are simply a different type of being.

Each of you is on an individual journey, yet your journeys combined are part of the journey of your world and of the Universe itself. Each step you take contributes. Each of your choices ripples out to affect those around you and in turn, those around them. You do not exist in isolation even at the times at which you feel the most isolated.

Know that hope and healing exist for you, and know that you are supported in these endeavors. Know, too, that although I may no longer communicate with as many humans in as direct a manner as previously, I am here to offer my support as well.

Share your knowledge and understanding with others, for you have essential contributions to make even if you believe otherwise. Trust that what you know and perceive is true, and that others will benefit from this truth. And be well and be loved.

ABOUT THE (HUMAN) AUTHOR

River Lightbearer (they/them) has been on a healing journey most of their adult life and has a passion for helping others heal and find their inner light. As a survivor of abuse and trauma, their heart is in guiding other survivors to gain ground in their journeys and create the lives they want to live. Their compassion, calming energy, and skills with the modality have supported numerous clients in their healing journeys.

Through their practice, River offers channeling and Chios® Energy Healing, both with a "side order" of mindset coaching, online/by distance to clients around the world.

River is a nonbinary eclectic Witch. In addition to this and other books under the River Lightbearer name, they also write or have written under the names Karenna Colcroft, KC Winter, Jo Ramsey, Kimberly Ramsey, and Kim Ramsey-Winkler. They are the mother to two nonbinary offspring and a son-in-law, as well as the grandmother to four wonderful children. River lives in Massachusetts with their husband. When not writing or serving other humans, River is the servant to two cats.

Learn more at https://riverlightbearer.com

Other currently or soon available books include:

WRITING AS RIVER LIGHTBEARER

Messages from Shiva vol. 1

The Guide Book

No Fault, No Blame: Channeled Encouragement for Trauma Survivors

WRITING AS KIM RAMSEY-WINKLER

The Yule Yikes (The Sabbat Series 1)

The Imbolc Incident (The Sabbat Series 2)

The Ostara Occurrence (The Sabbat Series 3)

The Beltane Business (The Sabbat Series 4)

The Midsummer Matter (The Sabbat Series 5)

www.ingramcontent.com/pod-product-compliance
Lightning Source LLC
LaVergne TN
LVHW010937110826
845149LV00013B/2641